Your Horoscope 2021

....

Aquarius

21 January – 19 February

igloobooks

Published in 2020
by Igloo Books Ltd
Cottage Farm
Sywell
NN6 0BJ
www.igloobooks.com

0820 001
2 4 6 8 10 9 7 5 3 1
ISBN 978-1-83852-314-5

Written by Belinda Campbell and Denise Evans

Cover design by Simon Parker
Edited by Bobby Newlyn-Jones

Printed and manufactured in China

CONTENTS
· · · · · · · · · · · · · · · · ·

INTRODUCTION

· · · · · · · · · · · · · · · · · ·

This 15-month guide has been designed and written to give a concise and accessible insight into both the nature of your star sign and the year ahead. Divided into two main sections, the first section of this guide will give you an overview of your character in order to help you understand how you think, perceive the world and interact with others and – perhaps just as importantly – why. You'll soon see that your zodiac sign is not just affected by a few stars in the sky, but by planets, elements, and a whole host of other factors, too.

The second section of this guide is made up of daily forecasts. Use these to increase your awareness of what might appear on your horizon so that you're better equipped to deal with the days ahead. While this should never be used to dictate your life, it can be useful to see how your energies might be affected or influenced, which in turn can help you prepare for what life might throw your way.

By the end of these 15 months, these two sections should have given you a deeper understanding and awareness of yourself and, in turn, the world around you. There are never any definite certainties, but with an open mind you will find guidance for what might be, and learn to take more control of your own destiny.

THE CHARACTER OF
THE WATER BEARER

. . . .

A rebel in the style of James Dean, with or without a cause, Aquarius is the Water Bearer sign of the zodiac that is here to give to their communities whilst also making waves. With the rebellious songs of the sixties in their ear, breaking tradition and challenging conventions is what this free-thinking air sign is all about. Whilst the songs of the 1960s might lay claim to the age of Aquarius, no one can quite agree on when this sign's astrological age begins or ends. An astrological age is thought to be close to 2000 years long and defined by the associated sign, so why is the age of Aquarius the one that everyone makes a song and dance about? Belonging to the eleventh house in the zodiac calendar that represents community and friendship, Aquarians and their astrological age are sure to influence and change up the whole world and everyone in it as this sign is about realising common goals, hopes and dreams for the future.

Co-ruled by rule-abiding Saturn and rebellious Uranus, Aquarians can be unapologetic when it comes to breaking tradition and will march to the beat of their own drum alone if they must, whether that's to the reggae beat of Bob Marley or the classical compositions of Mozart. Born in the middle of winter, fixed Aquarians may be set in their way of thinking, rightly or wrongly. With a positive energy, Aquarians can be wonderful at acting on what they believe. Aquarian activists Rosa Parks with her Montgomery Bus Boycott and Yoko Ono with her bed-ins for peace show how this sign can act against injustices. Aquarians are known for being progressive thinkers, with an eye fixed firmly on the future, which is perhaps why technological advancements are often closely linked with this futuristic sign. With Aquarians' devotion to their social responsibility and the speed at which technology is sky-rocketing, the age of Aquarius may well be in full swing as social media activism, or hashtivism, for example in movements like #TimesUp which continue to gather followers globally. With influential philanthropists and activists like Aquarians Ellen DeGeneres and Oprah Winfrey belonging to this star sign, the voice of Aquarius is sure to be heard for decades to come.

THE WATER BEARER

Despite being an Air sign, it is the giving Water Bearer that symbolises Aquarius. Ruled by Saturn who was named after the Roman god of agriculture, Aquarius' symbol of the Water Bearer shows the eternal current of positive energy that flows from this sign and helps the world to grow. The gifts of the Water Bearer can be numerous, but this Air sign is likely to influence society most substantially through their progressive thoughts and ideas. Aquarians can be visionaries, and this air sign's alternative way of thinking combined with their outgoing nature means that others are likely to listen to what they have to say. Although not everyone may agree with the rebel-minded Aquarius, this futuristic thinker is usually ahead of their time, their symbol of the Water Bearer suggests that what this sign will bring to the world will be given with the best of intentions for the goal of a brighter future.

SATURN AND URANUS

The second largest planet in the solar system, Saturn stands out as loud and proud as its co-ruled sign Aquarius. Belonging to the eleventh house of community, this Saturn ruled sign will likely take their social responsibility extremely seriously and may focus all their hard work into building a community that they believe to be just and fair. With the authority of Saturn co-guiding this sign, their fixed way of thinking can at times come across as a little preachy or superior, so this air sign should try to always listen and remain open-minded. Co-ruled by radical Uranus, Aquarians may be all about change and liberation from the rules of Saturn. Uranus is known for its off-kilter axis which could go a long way to explaining the alternative and unconventional traits that some Aquarians can display. Saturn's size and Uranus' unique tilt make these two planets stand out in the solar system and could act as a reminder to all belonging to this extraordinary sign that Aquarians were born to be a little different.

ELEMENTS, MODES AND POLARITIES

Each sign is made up of a unique combination of three defining groups: elements, modes and polarities. Each of these defining parts can manifest themselves in good and bad ways and none should be seen as a positive or a negative – including the polarities! Just like a jigsaw puzzle, piecing these groups together can help illuminate why each sign has certain characteristics and help us find a balance.

ELEMENTS

Fire: Dynamic and adventurous, signs with fire in them can be extroverted. Others are naturally drawn to them because of the positive light they give off, as well as their high levels of energy and confidence.

Earth: Signs with the earth element are steady and driven with their ambitions. They make for a solid friend, parent or partner due to their grounded influence and nurturing nature.

Air: The invisible element that influences each of the other elements significantly, air signs will provide much-needed perspective to others with their fair thinking, verbal skills and key ideas.

Water: Warm in the shallows and freezing as ice. This mysterious element is essential to the growth of everything around it, through its emotional depth and empathy.

MODES

Cardinal: Pioneers of the calendar, cardinal signs jump-start each season and are the energetic go-getters.

Fixed: Marking the middle of the calendar, fixed signs firmly denote and value steadiness and reliability.

Mutable: As the seasons end, the mutable signs adapt and give themselves over gladly to the promise of change.

POLARITIES

Positive: Typically extroverted, positive signs take physical action and embrace outside stimulus in their life.

Negative: Usually introverted, negative signs value emotional development and experiencing life from the inside out.

AQUARIUS IN BRIEF

The table below shows the key attributes of Aquarians.
Use it for quick reference and to understand more about this fascinating sign.

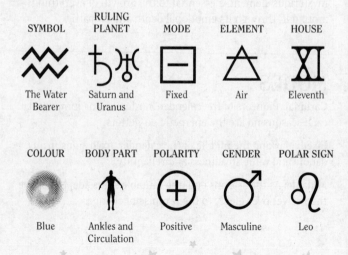

SYMBOL	RULING PLANET	MODE	ELEMENT	HOUSE
The Water Bearer	Saturn and Uranus	Fixed	Air	Eleventh

COLOUR	BODY PART	POLARITY	GENDER	POLAR SIGN
Blue	Ankles and Circulation	Positive	Masculine	Leo

ROMANTIC RELATIONSHIPS

· · · · · · · · · · · · · · · · · ·

Aquarians can be some of the friendliest and most alluring of all people and are unlikely to be short of admirers. They may have a laid-back approach to finding a partner, and if they are in a relationship can even seem aloof, but devotion is usually steadfast with this fixed sign. If an Aquarian is not overly emotional with their partner and is much happier to exchange thoughts and ideas than feelings, it is not necessarily because they are not emotionally invested in the relationship. A closed-off Aquarius could struggle with a water sign partner and likewise, water signs might not warm to the cool exterior of this air sign. Warm and passionate fire signs are sure to raise this air sign's temperature and as these elements share a positive outgoing energy, plenty of common interests could be shared. As is the case with many air signs, their love can feel like a trip to the heavens or a painful plummet to Earth. But even if this sign falls out of love, the friendships that they form can be so firm that they can withstand a break-up and be the rule breakers that do in fact stay friends with their exes.

Whilst being highly independent, Aquarians are all about teamwork so can truly thrive in a loving relationship so long as it stems from a firm friendship and mutual beliefs. This giving Water Bearer sign may struggle to give up their prized individualism in exchange for a partnership, and their fixed attitude can give them a stubborn edge that makes them resistant to accepting any dramatic changes to their lifestyle. A partner that understands their Aquarian's desire to remain autonomous and is fully accepting of their uniqueness is one that this sign should try and hold on to. A jealous or possessive lover is a big no-no for this free spirit. Aquarians who want to let love into their lives should understand that change is inevitable and what can feel like an upheaval to their independence is more of a loving revolution.

ARIES: COMPATIBILITY 3/5

Two signs known for their admirable quality of being a good friend to all, Aries and Aquarius should have a good solid foundation of friendship to base their romantic relationship on. This coupling of air and fire will always make for a fuelled love. Independence is key for keeping your Aquarius lover happy, so Aries should be careful with trying to control the relationship or forcing Aquarius to commit too soon. Whilst these two signs have many things in common, it will be discovering each other's differences that will be essential in keeping both partners interested in this relationship.

TAURUS: COMPATIBILITY 1/5

Taurus and Aquarius aren't an obvious match on paper – it's unlikely that these two will find each other on a matchmaking website! The core differences between these signs makes a romantic spark unlikely but should not be ruled out. Aquarius is partly ruled by the planet Uranus, symbolising rebellion and change, i.e. some Taureans' worst nightmare. For the easy life-seeking Taurus who likes what they know, the travel-lusting Aquarius can be hard to keep up with. However, these two signs are both fixed and have the potential to make each other stronger if they remain open to change.

GEMINI: COMPATIBILITY 4/5

The individualist sign Aquarius and Twin sign Gemini can make for a compatible trio. Born in the eleventh house that signifies community and friendship, Aquarians thrive in groups and will be a fantastic partner to social butterfly Gemini. The mutable nature of Geminis will mean that they are happy to follow their Aquarian fixed lover's lead which will likely bring a steadiness to the relationship. Being both positive and air signs, these two will have plenty in common. With a Gemini's love for change and an Aquarian's need for progress, these two could create a bright and revolutionary future together.

CANCER: COMPATIBILITY 1/5

The rebellious Aquarius and security seeking Cancer are not always an obvious match romantically. Whilst their core character differences may be the cause of arguments, if these two can find common interests that can cement a foundation for friendship then love could still bloom. If Cancer can help intellectual Aquarius give themselves emotionally to a partner, then both could mutually benefit from this unlikely but special meeting of the heart and mind. Find common ground to share and foreign lands to explore and Aquarius and Cancer could find a lasting love together.

LEO: COMPATIBILITY 5/5

Aquarius is the air sign that sparks the embers of Leo's
fire element into full blaze. Opposites on the calendar,
this combination of shared positive energy, fixed attitudes
and complimentary elements make Leo and Aquarius two
individuals that were astrologically made for each other. These
unique characters can be guilty of feeling superior to others
so may need to remind themselves to treat each other as their
rightful equals. Foremost, this is a friendship sprung from fun
and crafted by a shared creativity. The visionary mind of Leo
combined with Aquarian ideals could have these two creating a
utopic life together.

VIRGO: COMPATIBILITY 2/5

Idealist Aquarius and realist Virgo may not be an obvious
match, but this couple can be very happy if they find key
ideas and goals to share. The organised Virgo will appreciate
the Saturn ruled part of Aquarius that represents structure
and order but less so their rebellious Uranus side who enjoys
throwing the rulebook out. Airy Aquarius and Mercury ruled
Virgo are both free thinkers and should be good at allowing
each other room to breathe in the relationship which both
parties will value in their partner. Optimistic Aquarius and
pragmatic Virgo will need to find a shared ambition to balance
out their stark differences.

LIBRA: COMPATIBILITY 5/5

When these two air signs of Aquarius and Libra fall in love, it can be a whirlwind romance. Ruled by Venus and Uranus, this may well be a rebellious or radical type of love. Libra is a cardinal sign and is quick to come up with ideas and Aquarian's mode is fixed so makes an ideal partner to actualise their Libra lover's plans; teamwork really is dreamwork for this outgoing positive couple. The ideals of an Aquarius paired with Libra's righteousness can form a couple that will break down boundaries and create their own rules to make their ideal future.

SCORPIO: COMPATIBILITY 1/5

Mysterious Scorpio and unique Aquarius may well find themselves attracted to one another, but the Scorpion and Water Bearer may need to work hard to keep their relationship off the rocks. Positive Aquarians are outgoing, and socialising in their communities is important but this is different for introverted Scorpios who tend to have a small and intimate circle of friends. Their modes are both fixed which means they can be resistant to changing their contrasting outlooks. If stable Scorpio can embrace this air sign's free spirited nature and rational Aquarius can provide the intimacy that Scorpio needs, then these two could find their happiness.

SAGITTARIUS: COMPATIBILITY 4/5

Placed two apart on the zodiac calendar, the positive energies of an Aquarian and Sagittarian can be a complimentary and exciting love match. The thrilling ideas of a Sagittarius combined with Aquarian's independent thinking can mean that these stimulating spouses will have plenty to talk about. The fire in Sagittarius brings an enthusiastic energy to the relationship and the fixed mode of Aquarius can help provide a focus to their ideas and bring them into fruition. Communal minded Aquarius and sociable Sagittarius will likely be at the heart of their shared communities and bring great meaning to each other's lives.

CAPRICORN: COMPATIBILITY 1/5

Both ruled by Saturn, Capricorns and Aquarians will usually have a good understanding of the rules of love. However, Aquarians are co-ruled by Uranus, so may rebel against the traditions that most Capricorns value. A Capricorn and an Aquarius can both be extremely independent people, which may be what attracts them to one another, and as a creative couple they can really bring out the best in each other. This is a union of strong personalities and beliefs that may struggle to find common ground due to their opposite negative and positive energies, although their differences and determination could be their success.

AQUARIUS: COMPATIBILITY 3/5

When two air signs fall in love, it is usually a kindred meeting of the minds, but they should remember to share their hearts too. What may have first started as a friendship, the relationship of two Aquarians is unlikely to be stuck in the mud with both parties interested in progressing their feelings further. As a couple they may challenge the norm and their love can certainly seem radical to outsiders. Both individuals can be guilty of being stubborn or superior so should try loosening up their fixed attitudes. If these two share the same vision their future can be thought provoking and innovative.

PISCES: COMPATIBILITY 2/5

Two very giving signs such as Pisces and Aquarius could happily give themselves to each other in love. Whilst an air and water sign may struggle to understand one another, an Aquarian's intellect combined with a Piscean's compassion can form a relationship that speaks to both the heart and head if flexibility and patience is practised by the pair. A fixed and mutable mode can be a complimentary match, so long as Aquarians don't try to bend the will of their accommodating Piscean partner. The bond that these two can share when at its best can be sincere and spiritually liberating.

FAMILY AND FRIENDS

·················

Having a friend in Aquarius is surely having a friend for life. Whether this faithful sign has seen their chums last week or last year, these friendly souls will happily pick up where they last left off. Despite their likeable positive natures, their original and unconventional thoughts can at times make it hard for this sign to relate to their family and friends. Whether the loved ones of an Aquarius believe in the same things as them or not, surrounding themselves with open-minded people who will listen to their vast and sometimes controversial ideas will help this sign form bonds. Befriending a mutable sign like a Piscean or Sagittarian who will usually welcome a change of perspective could help Aquarians air their ideas freely and without judgment. For an intellectual chat or non-stop gossip, air signs like Libra and Gemini will always be happy to exchange ideas and chat endlessly with their Aquarian friend. Born in the eleventh house of friendship and community, being a member of a club or society is where Aquarians can feel most at home. There can be a secret side to Aquarius, some will certainly value their privacy, so perhaps a secret society or hanging out in a bar off the beaten track will be where to find this sign catching up with friends.

Aquarius' uniqueness could extend to their choice of home as this sign may find that they do not feel comfortable in a traditional setting such as a two-up two-down terraced house. Instead, they may feel more at home in a converted barn or church, or whatever perhaps best suits their one-off personality. Inside an Aquarian's home, their choice of interior is likely to continue to reflect their utterly unique personality; think eclectic and antique trinkets rather than Swedish

flat-pack furniture. Wherever this nomadic character decides
to settle, building a social network will be key to them and
they will no doubt be a positive pillar in their community.
Symbolised by the Water Bearer, Aquarians are intent on
making their community flourish and their giving and friendly
ways will usually have them working in a team for the greater
good. This Water Bearer might be found raising money for
their local watering hole or at the local council meeting
speaking their mind on how to best improve their local area
for the benefit of everyone.

When it comes to the family of an Aquarian, they will always
try to work as a team. Born in the eleventh house where
teamwork is key, Aquarians may be the one that encourages
each member of the family to vocalise their thoughts and
have a vital input into the way they function as a household.
As with their own life, Aquarians may favour an alternative
path for their children also. Home schooling may be an
Aquarian's preference if they find that their local schools are
too traditional for their liking. Aquarians will not want their
children to miss out on group activities so enrolling their child
in sports or other social clubs could be a priority. However, as
with any functional community, the voice of everyone will be
heard in an Aquarian's home and their children may have the
deciding vote or at least a valid input.

MONEY AND CAREERS

....

Being a certain star sign will not dictate the type of career
that you have, although the characteristics that fall under
each sign could help you identify the areas in which you could
potentially thrive. Conversely, to succeed in the workplace, it is
just as important to understand what you are good at as it is to
know what you are less brilliant at so that you can see the areas
in which you will need to perhaps work harder to achieve your
career and financial goals.

When it comes to money, Aquarians are usually far more
interested in the exchange of ideas than of cash. If an Aquarian
is money focused it will generally be because they want to help
their community in some way. To their friends and family,
Aquarius is known for their seemingly endless generosity and
this Water Bearer will come to parties with their arms full of
wine and treats for all. This sign is normally fixated on doing
things for the benefit of their fellow human so raising funds
for a local charity or donating their money to help restore a
nearby youth hostel are the types of projects that this giving
sign may like to spend their money on. Aquarians won't
typically be satisfied with donating just their money to the
good of the community and may find that their vocation is
working as a social worker or in another public sector where
they believe they can best serve their community and make
a difference, like human rights lawyer Amal Clooney, equal
rights campaigner Rosa Parks or suffragette Susan B. Anthony.
Aquarians want to make their communities better places and
make a difference for everyone.

As an air sign, a career that stretches their mind should be
well suited to an Aquarian. This futuristic sign could be set

on inventing the next world changing invention, theory, or technological advancement like Aquarians Thomas Edison or Charles Darwin. So innovative and outspoken is this sign that people are certainly inclined to listen to them in the workplace, even if their colleagues don't quite agree with their unique perspective. With Saturn by their side, Aquarians will usually be highly devoted to their work responsibilities and can be some of the most reliable and hard-working of signs. The authority given to this sign by Saturn could help Aquarians become a highly successful team manager or commanding boss of their own company, like Duncan Bannatyne. Their positive energy can be a stimulating force in the office and born in the eleventh house makes them both inspiring leaders and energetic team players – look at famous Aquarians Abraham Lincoln or Franklin D. Roosevelt to see how this sign can take charge and inspire people even in the trickiest of situations.

Whilst you can't always choose who you work with, it can be advantageous to learn about colleagues' key characteristics through their star signs to try and work out the best ways of working with them. Feeling the influence of radical Uranus can make it hard for Aquarians to follow someone else's rules, so their relationships with managers and bosses could be challenging at times if they do not share the same ethos. Born in the first house that represents the self, Aries could be a colleague that jars with the community minded Aquarius, whilst fellow air sign Libra could be the pioneering ideas seeking boss that gels well with Aquarius.

HEALTH AND WELLBEING

· · · · · · · · · · · · · · · · · ·

Another way in which this air sign can help clear their mind is by making sure that their environments are both peaceful and functional. Ensuring that their element of air and energy can flow freely throughout their household may be an Aquarian's priority so introducing the Chinese practice of feng shui into their home and office space could help restore some harmony.

Associated with blood circulation, an adrenaline fuelled sport that gets an Aquarian's blood pumping could be how this energetic sign likes to stay fit and healthy. This alternative air sign might literally be in their element taking on daring sports like base jumping or paragliding. Or if heights aren't an Aquarian's thing, skiing or snowboarding off piste somewhere a little different in the world might be more suited to this unconventional sign. After an active day on the slopes, a little *après ski* sauna will no doubt be where Aquarians make a beeline for in order to give their tired muscles and blood circulation that extra boost.

Having a healthy cholesterol level is essential for everyone wanting to live a long and healthy life, but it may be something that this sign is more keenly aware of to keep their associated body system of blood circulation thriving. Eating healthily is a great way to feel healthier and a proven way to naturally lower a high cholesterol, so if this is a concern for any star sign, reducing their intake of foods that are high in saturated fats such as red meat and cheese is always a good place to start. Making a few adjustments to diet, such as ordering the tuna steak rather than the beef, should boost the body with healthier omega three fats and have any sign, Aquarius included, feeling much healthier. Aquarians should try not being a total stranger to their local GP, even if they prefer to practise alternative home remedies to battle the flu rather than get their annual jab, and always seek professional guidance if they have concerns about their health.

Mental health should be tended to just as readily as physical health and, as for any air sign, having a happy and clear mind is essential to an Aquarian's wellbeing. If an Aquarian's head is feeling clogged up with stress or worries, their usually innovative and free flowing ideas can feel blocked which can compound an air sign's anxiety. Identifying the root of the problem could be the first step as the cause of anxiety may or may not be obvious. By tackling issues candidly, an Aquarian can then plan the most practical route to a happy solution, which could include turning to their beloved community, be it a neighbour or sibling, and asking for help.

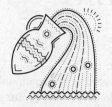

Aquarius

DAILY FORECASTS
for 2020

OCTOBER

Thursday 1st

Happy Full Moon in Aries. This Full Moon highlights what you've learned with regard to new communications, and it's also a great moment to have a look at your environment and take a stock-check. What's worth holding onto and what should you release to move ahead enthusiastically?

Friday 2nd

The Venus in Virgo transition will be an interesting one this year as it will allow you some of the seeds you set out to grow. You focus on being useful and may have access to further resources. Venus is about money so some cash might come your way.

Saturday 3rd

Venus connects to the Moon in Taurus, and bringing supportive energy coming from your home and family sector. It could be you stocking up the resources to sustain your family and maybe a new home. However, this is definitely some good news and a win on both sides.

Sunday 4th

Why do you like to work on Sundays? Maybe it's your way of keeping things unpredictable, although everyone who knows you will expect that already. This can still bring up conflict with your family, however, so how do you want to handle it this time?

Monday 5th

Pluto, the planet of transformation, destruction and resurrection is moving direct again. You can be assured that you've broken enough structures for now and can focus on using the scattered pieces in a new way. Today's mood is about seeking comfort and pleasure, and possibly good food.

Tuesday 6th

The Moon is in Gemini, while the Sun is in Libra. Get out a pen and paper, brushes, pencils and start to create. You don't need to focus on a specific outcome, just do it for the sheer joy, and you will be delighted with what you can create if there's no pressure at all.

Wednesday 7th

Your family may have a surprise in store, or something is revealed at work that has an unexpected effect on your home life. This could be about a relocation, business travel or a promotion. Don't rush the decision and if you can, ponder it over the next month and during the upcoming Mercury retrograde.

Thursday 8th

The Moon is moving into Cancer and ringing tension in relation to the Sun and Capricorn. There are likely to be mood swings, and you may feel somehow busy all the time. Balance is today's goal so stick to routines and activities that add to your self-care.

. . . .

Friday 9th

It's the second of three discussions Mars between Pluto. This time Mars is retrograde and Pluto is moving ahead, so try to adjust your actions to the ongoing transformation. You're acting more carefully and possibly differently from your first attempt, so act upon your deepest desires.

Saturday 10th

Venus is in an easy conversation with Uranus, and you might receive some money or be able to access some resources provided by your family. It's an unexpected blessing, and you're not yet sure how to handle it as everything has happened quickly. Breathe and count to ten.

Sunday 11th

Are you ready to expand your vision? The Sun and Jupiter are in a challenging meeting and they ask you to surpass yourself. This is a blessing in disguise because most often we need to overcome an obstacle to realise how much more we are capable of.

Monday 12th

The Moon is in Leo, and you enjoy spending time with your partner and at least for today don't consider anything else more important. It's rare to have your undivided attention, so why not make it more special with a generous gift?

Tuesday 13th

The Sun is in a tug-of-war with Mars retrograde. Many options seem to be available, but which is the right one to act upon? Staying with the old or trying your luck somewhere new? With the Moon in Virgo, you look at all the needs your family has and try to create a plan.

Wednesday 14th

The topic of your work and legacy needs further investigation. There might still be things hidden from you, and you need to rethink, investigate and ponder. Mercury retrograde is here to help you out and give you the perfect setup to do that. Three weeks to gain clarity lie ahead.

Thursday 15th

The Sun is in another discussion with Pluto. Are you already making use of your power and adjusting your vision? Or are you still playing too small? Dare to dream big. The effort is needed anyway so why go for something small if you could also achieve the real deal?

Friday 16th

Happy New Moon in Libra. This is the perfect time to review and see where you are. Perhaps you could make a mind-map to work out what truly inspires you. Put it somewhere in sight, at best a place where you can see it daily.

Saturday 17th

This Saturday, your mind and heart align, and you come to a place of inner peace and stillness. There is still a lot to figure out, but at least you don't feel torn apart any longer. Something previously hidden might come to the surface, and it is likely a critical moment for your upcoming decision.

Sunday 18th

The Sun has lots of discussions these days, and this one is with Saturn. It's about sticking with the rules and making sure that all dreams have a chance to be realised. You will need patience because you cannot rush the process, but if you show up and take one step at a time, the rewards will be granted.

Monday 19th

There's exciting energy as Jupiter is in a fluid connection to Venus and in a stressful one with Mars. You're making plans on how to expand in an organised fashion but aren't yet ready to act upon them, which can bring frustration. A good counterbalance is to meet with your friends and have some fun.

Tuesday 20th

Mercury retrograde is now facing your co-ruler Uranus, as if to ask for another big revelation or insight. It might be a perfect time to discuss the upcoming possible changes with your family to consider their point of view. It helps you to see everything from another perspective.

Wednesday 21st

The overall tone is severe today, and you are mainly busy with yourself. A good vibration is coming from Venus in a harmonious connection to Pluto. This is about being able to use your power appropriately for a more significant cause and to make use of the resources at hand.

Thursday 22nd

The Sun is entering your area of vocation, legacy and career. A major decision may come up during that transit. Patience is a virtue, and you might need to breathe deep often because you desperately want to move ahead but it's not the time. Use the chance to rework and refigure the things you have already worked on.

Friday 23rd

It's perfect energy for a Friday. You're able to focus on work in the morning and once your leisure time arrives the energy opens up and you have time to experiment and feel as independent as your heart desires. The Moon is in your sign so just enjoy the energy in alignment with yourself.

Saturday 24th

Another solution is knocking at your door. You might have found new resources that you can invest in building your new structures. With Saturn and Venus both in Earth energy and in signs that deal with responsibility, discernment and practicability, you have green lights for moving ahead.

Sunday 25th

Mercury is back in the heart of the Sun, waiting to receive insights about your career situation. With the Moon in Pisces and the easy connection to Scorpio, it's possible that your dreams have some messages and ideas rising from the depth of your subconscious into your consciousness.

Monday 26th

Dreamlife is enhanced and so is your desire to have a bit of magic in your life. It would be a great time to watch a movie, read a book or go to the theatre. Nothing major is happening, which is a welcome shift and allows you to take a breath.

Tuesday 27th

More magic and more rest, please. The energy is continuously chill, and you can lie around and dream about utopia without feeling guilty. Make sure you still follow your routines to stay grounded and know that tomorrow's energy will be very different. So enjoy the time to retreat.

Wednesday 28th

Mercury retrogrades back into Libra, so it seems like you need to take a look at your long term aims and make some adjustments. Venus is also moving into Libra, where she loves to be, so you can be sure lots of harmony is coming your way. It's time to focus on the people that accompany you.

Thursday 29th

Connect to your neighbours or family today as there might be an important message or hint hidden in the conversations you conduct. This hint will help you out with further adjustments, and with regards to the decisions you have to make about your career and the environment you want to live in.

Friday 30th

Lots of Earth energy is around and after dealing with issues in the morning, the energy eases, and you can have a beautiful and chilled-out evening within the family circle. Going out for a family dinner would be an excellent way to add some extravagance to your day.

Saturday 31st

If you've been seeking to try something new, or to make changes in your life, then today might be the perfect time to begin. The Full Moon is likely to present new opportunities from turning over a new leaf to unexpected invitations. Be sure to look within for answers if you're unsure which step to take.

NOVEMBER

Sunday 1st

There's an unexpected development happening in your career and home situation. But you're full of an undeniable optimism that the solution will present itself. Good! Don't allow others to alter your perspective. They might not be open-minded enough to see the situation resolve.

Monday 2nd

The safety you experience in your family is built on a solid foundation and will last and carry you through no matter where you go. You just need to be aware that being rooted is not the same as being stuck. When the Moon shifts into Gemini this evening it's time to have some joy and laughter.

Tuesday 3rd

It's important to know who is on your team. Who are the people who thrive on your ideas and vice versa? Who are the ones that can dream the same dream as you? Make sure you spend time relating those who support you and be supportive in return.

Wednesday 4th

Congratulations on having had such a hard look at your career choices and opportunities. You did enough rethinking, and Mercury is now moving direct. With the Moon on its current trajectory, you feel ready to make a proper choice and set sails to the future.

Thursday 5th

It's possible that you feel afraid to follow your vision. What if you find yourself all on your own? What if you cannot stick to your routines or fail to nurture yourself? There's no need to be afraid. You have the flexibility to create routines in a different environment.

Friday 6th

What would you actually have to change in order to function in a new environment? What's necessary for you to feel safe and nurtured? Consider internal and external security. What's required to make you feel comfortable? Everyone has their own requirements to feel at home. Which ones are yours?

Saturday 7th

This weekend you might pack up with your partner and go on a trip. See something different and making sure you are seen too. It won't be the super romantic, just a snuggling in the sheets style of weekend, but more about visiting museums or even attending an event.

Sunday 8th

Where and how you show up at today's event could be important for your public image. You could run into somebody by coincidence, or it could also be possible that you merely forgot to tell your partner that this is a business meeting? This might cause some tension. Let your charm play and your heart show.

Monday 9th

Monday morning and you are still high as a kite from the weekend's energy, which was a real boost to your self-esteem. It might be a little hard to focus in the morning, but in the afternoon you are back on track and can start to take care of some important details.

Tuesday 10th

Today, Mercury is back on the edge of Libra, so you can have some final thoughts about your vision and then it's all about integrating them in your career and legacy. It's a significant chance, and you are the only person who knows if you dare to take it. But do you want to ask "what if"?

Wednesday 11th

You have an analytical look at the current situation and are able to commit, as you see everything is in perfect alignment and you're almost ready to get up and go. It has been a long time coming, but you feel like something is shifting soon and you are right.

Thursday 12th

The best things come in threes. This is the final meeting of Jupiter and Pluto, this time under Saturn's beady eye. Now they get it right, and you're finally able to unite your deepest desires with your highest intentions and the sky's the limit.

Friday 13th

It's a day of adjustments before the energy shifts once more to your legacy and career. It's possible that you spend this weekend contemplating, but you never know what you will come up with. Once you're in your creative genius mode, you dive in deep.

Saturday 14th

Finally, the day has come. You've been so frustrated during these last months where you felt stuck and like you couldn't move ahead, but instead had to redo lots of things. Now Mars is moving direct again. A big relief and time to make the change happen.

Sunday 15th

Happy New Moon in Scorpio. It's perfect and seems to be the divinely guided new beginning to set you up for your career, vocation and legacy. Set your goals regarding your public image, the impact you want to have in the world and how you want to be perceived.

Monday 16th

It's time for a little break. You're not always so committed and willing to do the work without taking a break, but that's with good reason as too much of what's seen as "hard work" just leaves you dry like a flower without water. Refresh by adding vision and creativity.

Tuesday 17th

Watch out! Mercury is back in opposition to your co-ruler and what comes up today will reveal the choice you've already made. With the Moon in the south, you're able to see which social circles you need to disconnect from. This choice doesn't come easy but is well considered.

Wednesday 18th

It's time for action: unbelievable, but true! Remember to act from a place of integrity and inner authority. You need to be willing to take full responsibility, put in every effort and be disciplined and show up every single day. The next month might feel like snail speed, but you are moving.

Thursday 19th

Today's energy is serious, constructive and vital. It's like a final and official approval. This can come from the outside like a boss or another authority figure, or it could be from your inner authority. Don't underestimate the effect your self-validation has. It is huge.

Friday 20th

Shake it up and shake yourself a little loose. Be a rebel today and allow yourself to do everything differently, just to mix things up. Even small changes can help you refresh yourself and see things from a new perspective. You'll probably have lots of ideas for things you could change.

Saturday 21st

Today's energy is beautiful and sees two significant shifts. The Sun is entering Sagittarius, willing to bring in your new tribe and is supported by Venus enhancing your work relationships. The Moon brings some necessary energy. Exciting times are ahead!

Sunday 22nd

Use this Sunday to hang loose, recharge and drift away in daydreams. Wear your comfiest clothes or something that adds a sense of magic to your day and escape into fantasy land, either with a book, movie or music. It could be a beautiful autumn day, so getting out in nature might be a good idea too.

Monday 23rd

Empathy and compassion are high. It's not a day for making tough choices but for listening carefully to what your fellow human beings have to say. You can read between the lines and hear what isn't being said. It might be difficult to differentiate which emotions are your own.

Tuesday 24th

You're still very tuned into the world around you. There might be lots of signs and synchronicities, you just need to see them and figure out what they mean. The universe is telling you that you're on the right path. Dreams can hold messages, so try to remember them as well as you can.

Wednesday 25th

Wouldn't it be nice to organise a little feast with your friends? You're willing to take the initiative and send the invitations. It should be a lovely meeting, and you'll have lots of inspiring conversations.

Thursday 26th

You're unstoppable today, ready to take various actions and focus on your goals and your development. You are able to control your mood swings and keep pushing forward, which might help your co-workers to do the same. Be bold and courageous!

Friday 27th

Venus in opposition to your co-ruler Uranus can make or break a deal. The deal is created when you feel safe and comfortable and will break if there's even the tiniest amount of distrust. If you're in, you're all in. Listen to your inner voice. It's whispering the answer all the time.

Saturday 28th

Nothing major is happening, you could say it's a usual Saturday, which actually makes it an unusual one for you, because how many ordinary Saturdays do you have? The most exciting thing could be reading a new book or watching a new movie. Relax!

Sunday 29th

Another laid-back day, at least speaking about outside appearances. There might be a family dinner or lunch which you enjoy, but inside there's something brewing. Mercury and Jupiter are in a harmonious connection which lights up your mood and expands your mind. Only the deep and complex themes are exciting today.

Monday 30th

The month ends with a partial Lunar Eclipse in Gemini. It's potent energy supported by a connection from Mercury to Saturn. Take a look at the last six months, you've taken many steps towards your future. It might have looked like nothing happened, but it was a lot. Kudos to you!

DECEMBER

· · · · · · · · · · · · · · · · · ·

Tuesday 1st

It's the beginning of the final month this year and wouldn't you think the energy would calm down? Major energy shifts are coming up, and you won't have a dull moment. The Moon is pointing towards the future while Mercury enters Sagittarius and you focus on the bigger picture and your tribe.

Wednesday 2nd

You're a little sensitive today and need to listen to your feelings. Maybe with all that excitement and everything you tried to figure out, you didn't take the time just to feel. Let all the emotions rise up today and do everything to make yourself feel comfortable.

Thursday 3rd

Consider what you learned about nurturing yourself this year. Some actions and routines proved more important than others. What do you want to learn and could you make a start now? You know all the answers, what works for you might not be what works for others.

Friday 4th

The Moon enters Leo later today and combines with the Sun and Mercury in Sagittarius. It's amazing energy for gatherings with friends and loved ones. You can have a lovely time, amazing conversations and tell tale after tale. You might end up being the entertainer at the party.

Saturday 5th

A little family conflict could disturb the otherwise peaceful Saturday mood. If you don't make mountains out of molehills, this can be resolved quickly. You will want to be out and about and spread some gifts in your neighbourhood. Neighbourly help clearly counts and is highly appreciated.

Sunday 6th

Focus on the love, any kind of love. Self-love, earthly love and divine and unconditional love. You want to spread some love today, and you can do best if you come from a place of trust. Focus on feeling, without trying to analyse how each emotion is defined.

Monday 7th

Something more tangible is on the table today. You do a check up on your finances and might figure out that there's more available than you thought. This is excellent news. You might take a second look to be sure, but then you allow gratitude to take over.

Tuesday 8th

It feels terrific to be set up, and you could burst with joy because of that. You're highly optimistic and might spread good vibrations for many people in your life. Memorise that feeling, this is what it feels like when you're in alignment within yourself.

Wednesday 9th

Be very cautious during the next few days. You could fall for illusions. If something seems to be too good to be true, it most likely is. All that glitters is not gold. There are some very well-done fakes, and there are also people wearing masks.

Thursday 10th

Watch out, there could still be some deception going on. If you follow your instincts and investigate, you can easily expose the person under suspicion. It will be harder to tell if you're the one deceiving yourself and falling for an illusion. Take a hard look at reality.

Friday 11th

It's time to say goodbye to some social circles and groups. They might have helped you out a lot, entertained you and broadened your mind, but on your new road you need some new people. Say goodbye properly, have an honourable, respectful ending and don't run away.

Saturday 12th

The Moon is meeting Venus, and you could have a final meet and greet with some of the people you are leaving behind. It's likely to be related to your work or legacy so it could be some co-workers or people from a club or a charity. Show your gratitude.

Sunday 13th

The Moon in Sagittarius is asking for engagement: you might be out and about and in meetings again. Save some time and think about your development and what you could teach others from your experience. You have achieved some wisdom, and you should not keep it to yourself.

Monday 14th

Happy New Moon in Sagittarius. This New Moon has a super optimistic vibe with Jupiter and Venus connected to it. You can set the intentions for your new adventure! Declare that you will look on the bright side of life and commit to the people supporting and joining you.

Tuesday 15th

Your optimism sparks your actions and Venus is now joining the other planets in Sagittarius. There's such a big emphasis of hope and faith and joyful energy, it's Christmas spirit at its best. You need to take a little time for yourself, and you'd better do it soon because so much is coming down the pipeline!

Wednesday 16th

It's unlikely that you'll find a state of calmness and peace today because the energy is so exciting and feels more like you fidget around on your chair. Find some time for meditation, a walk outside can be meditative as well. Connect to your core and know you have access to your inner power.

Thursday 17th

Saturn is leaving Capricorn! He's now entering your sign, and this is a massive turning point. This transit will keep you busy during the next two-and-a-half years, and it's the beginning of a new era. You can be the reformer and revolutionary you were born to be.

Friday 18th

Mercury is in the heart of the Sun for the final time in 2020. That this happens in Sagittarius will only unleash more hope and optimism. It's a beautiful set up for a new year. The Moon's position makes it seem like New Year has come early.

Saturday 19th

Are you ready for the next massive shift? Yes, there's more to come. Jupiter is on the final degree of Capricorn and can't wait to get out of there and slip into Aquarius. This has been an uncomfortable space for him, dealing with lots of restriction, but at least he could share his wisdom and you learned a lot.

Sunday 20th

One more biggie before Christmas. Jupiter in Aquarius is ready to give you a boost in self-confidence and growth you haven't seen for a while. Saturn is here waiting for him, and as they both join forces, they set you up for significant achievements, improvements, inventions and the revolution.

Monday 21st

The Sun enters Capricorn. For you, this brings a focus on self-reflection, but this next year it will be so much easier for you, as there is only Pluto sitting in that area and all the other weight has gone. You can sigh in relief and get ready for a relatively calm Capricorn season.

Tuesday 22nd

All these shifts and changes have been quite a lot to deal with, and you don't know if you're coming or going. Take a breath and think about Christmas. Is there anything you need to prepare or buy? Focus on something small for now, do your best and don't stress out.

Wednesday 23rd

This is the third and final time that Mars and Pluto square each other this year. It's about acting on your deepest desires and moving in the right direction. As both planets move forward, you are finally progressing, too. Find the time to meditate and listen to your inner voice to guide you.

Thursday 24th

Christmas Eve is here, and you'll most likely want to spend this with your family and loved ones. As the Moon is in Taurus, everything is set up to be comfortable and classy. It's likely to be calm, the only thing to remember is you can also agree to disagree.

Friday 25th

Merry Christmas! The Moon is crossing your co-ruler, and Uranus is always good for a surprise. Maybe a family member has some happy news. Christmas gifts count as a surprise too so it will be a peaceful day with jolly conversations and hopefully amazing food to indulge in.

Saturday 26th

Boxing day, and you need a little space to retreat. Take some time for yourself if possible. When you're around others, put the focus on the spirit of Christmas and feel not only the love but also the magic. It's a day to be peaceful and relax.

Sunday 27th

Even though it's Sunday, you've had enough rest and want some fun and action. You could want to go out, dance or start to dive into creative endeavours. At least, if you find the time, as your phone could constantly be ringing, and you'll probably agree to some spontaneous visits.

Monday 28th

The Sun is in a harmonious connection to your co-ruler Uranus. An unexpected door is opening for you and all you need to do is walk through. This is in alignment with your future path so grab your luck by the scruff of its neck.

Tuesday 29th

Happy Full Moon in Cancer. Interesting that the year started and ends with a Cancer Full Moon. Look at how much you evolved emotionally during that year. It's a great deal to feel safe within yourself. Well done, and keep it up next year.

Wednesday 30th

There needs to be compassion and surrender. You cannot always push ahead, sometimes you need to trust the process and that there are higher forces involved. You have learned a lot but never forget that even though you are open-minded, you cannot see the entire picture. There will always be something hidden.

Thursday 31st

Welcome to New Year's Eve. What a year it has been! Massive, profound, challenging, intense, exciting and you surpassed yourself. When you move forward to your future, never forget the lessons learned. Great things are awaiting you, and you can make a huge difference in the upcoming year.

Aquarius

DAILY FORECASTS
for 2021

JANUARY

. . . .

Friday 1st

Happy New Year and welcome to 2021. Last night a Full Moon in your health and duties sector may have seen you caring for everyone and hosting a great party. Your love and insistence that everyone is happy put you in the spotlight. What a great way to start the year.

Saturday 2nd

You may now make use of the Moon's energy to connect with a lover or partner. Those who are magnetic and charismatic attract you and share their warmth. At these times it's important for you to find that your own voice matches those of the most important people in your life.

Sunday 3rd

The Moon moves to your intimacy sector. Once more you're looking after family and ensuring that everything is in place. You love to make it easy for others to be around you. As a perfect host, you may be gathering your family close for a last-minute celebration.

Monday 4th

Your planner is already filling up with dates, engagements and places to go. Be careful that you don't plan unrealistic activities or those which will cost too much. You may already be letting money fly through your fingers. Keep it real, dream it into being, but manifest the finances too.

Tuesday 5th

Mercury and Pluto meet today in your hidden sector. It's likely that you've been constantly reinventing yourself or doing your important inner work for several years now. Mercury will receive his new mission and you'll learn what your work is to be for this year. Get ready.

Wednesday 6th

Mars spends his final day in your communications sector. You may find that you're networking aggressively or rushing to finish a job that was possibly begun last year. Finish up all the important details before starting on something new. Be careful not to get too bossy with others.

Thursday 7th

Mars shifts into your family sector. Be prepared for a high level of activity or motivation while he's here. There may be many things going on in your home environment. This will be a good time for home improvements, money-making schemes or family gatherings.

Friday 8th

The Moon and Mercury are squaring off and you may find that your emotions are knocked off balance. You may desire to get stuck into a work project but find that your mind wanders off to more personal problems. This is Mercury awakening you to your new mission this year.

53

Saturday 9th

Mercury flies into your own sign and you put your innermost thoughts to the test. Venus glides into your hidden sector to help you do this with due care and attention to yourself. Be wild, be radical but be cautious. Don't make yourself vulnerable today as you will fall at the first hurdle.

Sunday 10th

Listen to the words of the wise today. You may meet someone who challenges your way of thinking. It's also possible that you meet a brand-new teacher who can guide you safely through what may feel like an empowering but tough time. The way is shown to you today.

Monday 11th

Your thoughts and speech are buoyant. An uplifted mood gets you through the day where you are positive and joyous. This may rub off onto those you meet today. Keep this up and you'll be off to a flying start this year. Believe in yourself.

Tuesday 12th

The Moon enters your hidden sector and you find that you're emotionally invested in making changes for the better. You may find the perfect teachers this year and will learn a lot. Don't worry about upsetting the status quo or even your family as all around you will benefit.

Wednesday 13th

A New Moon occurs in your hidden sector. This gives you a great opportunity to commit to self-improvement and working on issues you have previously struggled with. You may feel defensive and a little reluctant to start what may be a life-changing journey. Trust in yourself and take small steps.

Thursday 14th

You may feel more vulnerable today. The Sun and Pluto meet and ask that you look at old ways of coping. Do they still meet your needs? The Moon dips into your own sign where you may be sensitive to how you are perceived. Speak your truth if requested to.

Friday 15th

Enjoy a peaceful day where you can truly be yourself. You may be looking for something unusual to do over the weekend. Saturn, your ruler, is teaching you the first lesson. Be your unique self but remember that what excites you may not interest others. Don't be dismayed by this.

Saturday 16th

Today may be surreal and floaty. It's possible to have a day of dreaming and switching off. Be mindful that you don't need substances to do this. Money may slip through your fingers if you are not careful. If you must make an impulse buy, do it on something lasting.

Sunday 17th

Jupiter in your sign squares off with Uranus in your family sector. You may find that your own needs conflict with those of your tribe and your peace is disturbed. The Moon meets Neptune and you may be drawn into unrealistic thinking or seek a spiritual outlet.

Monday 18th

Today you may be fired up and slightly aggressive. Use that aggression to get things done and be productive. There's a chance that you see conflict in the family, but you can override this and be assertive. People will listen to your authority and give you respect.

Tuesday 19th

The Sun enters your sign today. This is your birthday month, happy birthday! It's easy to communicate your wishes to others as you have the gift of the gab with Mercury in your sign. However, Venus is reminding you to take care of your own needs too. Self-neglect is possible.

Wednesday 20th

Mars and Uranus meet in your family sector. Expect surprises as this volatile duo can cause disruption and conflict. Alternatively, this can be a time of high energy where everyone helps to complete a project. Used wisely, this energy can move mountains. Avoid volcanic outbursts if you can.

Thursday 21st

The Moon catches up with Mars and Uranus. Whatever it is that's coming to boiling point will now have your emotions invested in it. Your feelings may be hurt if this has become a negative event. If it's positive, then you are putting your heart and soul into great things.

Friday 22nd

Be mindful of outdated coping mechanisms today. The recent volatile energy may have left you with a realisation that something must change. What didn't work out for you? Maybe it's time to take a good look at how you might start to approach things differently.

Saturday 23rd

The Moon enters your creativity sector and gives you a chance to unwind with something you love doing. You may have many artistic projects going on and have difficulty choosing one. Venus and Neptune make a nice connection to help you soothe yourself with whatever activity you choose today.

Sunday 24th

Today the Sun meets your ruler, Saturn. This marks the importance of listening to teachers, elders and leaders. An opportunity may present itself to you. This will enhance your self-improvement and is worth taking. It could well be the first small step to greater things. Do the responsible thing.

Monday 25th

Mars and Jupiter square off today. Jupiter makes everything bigger so expect your Mars drive to assert yourself and get things done to be larger than usual. The downside is that this energy may make you more aggressive than driven. By evening you may wish to retreat and have alone time.

Tuesday 26th

You have a very good sense of your duties and obligations. Ego clashes are likely today, but you have the ability to be the peacemaker and gather hurt people around you. Your love and compassion may be needed. Try cooking a favourite meal and being a parent figure.

Wednesday 27th

You may notice that today is all about what you do for others. This may be another thing that needs to change or be tweaked a little. It's likely that you feel some resistance or resentment towards those who need your attention. If you feel selfish today, indulge your emotional side but don't overdo it.

Thursday 28th

A Full Moon occurs in your relationship sector. This is a huge spotlight on your closest relationships and the patterns within. You may feel as if you're on stage or being judged so show your best side off. This may be a completion of some sort.

Friday 29th

The Sun meets Jupiter in your sign. Your ego may be huge today. You may be narcissistic and a show-off. Alternatively, you may have the right to be proud of yourself now. This may be a showcase of your own talents and skills. Whichever it is for you, it will be big.

Saturday 30th

Mercury goes retrograde tomorrow in your sign. Use today to make all the necessary preparations. Back up all your devices, double check travel plans and be mindful not to sign commitments for the next three weeks. Communications skills will be needed now to avoid misunderstandings.

Sunday 31st

Mercury retrograde begins. The Moon sits opposite Neptune and you may feel drained of energy. It isn't possible to get any clarity today and you must be adaptable as things will change often. Check every detail and then check again. Go with the flow as this will be easier for you.

FEBRUARY

....

Monday 1st

Venus enters your sign today. This should help to take the
edge off Mercury's mishaps. You may still have some conflict
between your own needs and those of the family. Look to other
cultures for some inspiration on how to put self-improvement
measures in place this year. You may find some balancing
influences here.

Tuesday 2nd

Put your family disputes to one side today. Other planetary
energy is more favourable. A teacher or elder may cross your
path and cause you to prick up your ears. You may have a
sudden yearning to expand your horizons and feel pulled
towards distant lands.

Wednesday 3rd

An intense day at work lets you show your leadership skills and
power through the day. Be scrupulous as the Moon makes its
first connection to Mercury retrograde. Mars and Venus are
not playing nicely so you may see some trouble between lovers
or opposite-sex family members. Males may be stubborn today.

Thursday 4th

Stay away from any drama you may come across in your family
sector. Jealousy or secretive behaviour may show itself now.
As the Moon opposes both Mars and Uranus you may be in for
a bumpy day. Remember that you can't please everyone all the
time. This isn't your job.

Friday 5th

Mercury challenges you to think on your feet today. A work issue may be problematic, and emails or messages may be misunderstood. You will need to get control of this before it gets out of hand. Pluto, who deals with permanent change, is rooting for you in your hidden sector.

Saturday 6th

Look to your wider groups this weekend as they will bring you joy and optimism. You may have friends far and wide, but you are excellent at keeping in touch with them all. Venus and Saturn meet and give you a game plan for looking after yourself safely.

Sunday 7th

A whimsical feeling may come over you and you think to times past when things were seemingly easier. This is idealistic thinking. You're allowed to reminisce but remember that you're here now, and things have moved on. Family members may bring you back to reality with a bump.

Monday 8th

Mercury is in the heart of the Sun today. Your job is to listen for messages, hints, gossip or symbols. Your hidden sector may begin to bring up material from your deepest parts for healing and improvement. You may be triggered today so be good to yourself.

Tuesday 9th

You will have a lot to think about today. You get a glimpse of your true north, your direction in life, from Neptune and have an unusual emotional pull towards it. However, Neptune needs you to dissolve something first. Pluto seconds this. What will you let go of now?

Wednesday 10th

The Moon dips into your sign and passes the planets in there. Now is the time where you may feel pushed and pulled in different directions but think of it as adjustment. This is where your learning will take place this year. Share your love but keep some for yourself too.

Thursday 11th

A New Moon in your sign is the perfect opportunity to make a commitment to yourself. Make plans, goals, set schedules and create a vision board. Let the revolution begin. Think big today as Venus meets Jupiter and this energy is filled with blessings you can access for the future.

Friday 12th

Your sector of finances and value is now visited by the young Moon. Here is where you may have unrealistic ideas about money and place value on intangible things. You must keep your feet on the ground and assess something's worth only if you can touch it, see it or spend it.

Saturday 13th

The Moon meets dreamy Neptune and you may desire a weekend of good music, dancing, food and company. You're inspired to connect with your friendships by offering them a break from their mundane lives as this will benefit you too. Mercury retrograde meets Venus and challenges your love life.

Sunday 14th

Stay with the dreamy, floaty feeling until evening then come back down to earth slowly. You will be ready to begin a new week in a very different frame of mind. Mercury's mischief may catch you out today so tread carefully and be vigilant. Rebellion is likely.

Monday 15th

You begin the week fired up and ready to engage in any way necessary. You may have too much energy and could get burnt out very quickly. The fiery Moon connects to both Saturn and Jupiter reminding you that you have responsibilities that need attention today. Go at a comfortable pace.

Tuesday 16th

This could be one of those days where you successfully put yourself first. Use the same amount of energy to take care of your own needs as you do for others. You may begin to see something falling away or changing deep in your psyche. It will be uncomfortable at first.

Wednesday 17th

Expect to feel some deep disturbances today which may rumble on for a while. You do your best to ensure that family life runs smoothly, to the minute even, but you're aware of something else. Saturn and Uranus are unearthing issues within the family that you must change.

Thursday 18th

The Sun enters your finance and values sector today. This may herald a month of blowing away cobwebs from your wallet and letting you have a good hard look at your money situation. You will be less likely to overspend now. Energy may be low when the Moon meets Mars.

Friday 19th

Like the perfect host, you have many chores to do within your family environment. You are expert at juggling everything and pulling people into line. If you need help, don't be too modest to ask for it. You may see some quarrels in your family of origin today.

Saturday 20th

Look at your long list of leisure activities and try to choose one to do this weekend. You may connect to groups of people you have not seen for a while. Your friendship groups are huge, and you may have many stories to share. Take time to laugh out loud today.

Sunday 21st

Mercury turns direct today. This will make you feel lighter and happier to make a commitment. Friends and social groups can bring you joy and take you with them on an adventure towards a future goal. Creatively, you are on top form today. Romance is highlighted too. This is a happy day.

Monday 22nd

The Moon creeps into your health and duties sector. You're happy to start the week and feel nurtured. Staying in your safety zone of routine will do you good. You may expect a nice surprise from your family or a great new idea which you can all pursue.

Tuesday 23rd

Emotional energy may catch you by surprise today. Music, poetry, romance, love and compassion will play a big part in making your day go well. You may have time to switch off and be looked after by another. Allow yourself to take time out and enjoy this.

Wednesday 24th

There may be a disruption to your happy mood today as you feel as if you are being manipulated or controlled. This is the Moon opposing Pluto in your hidden sector. Note what the triggers are. This may be something coming up for healing. Embrace it and deal with it now.

Thursday 25th

The Moon enters your relationship sector but also opposes all the planets in your own sign. This may make you uncertain about a lover or cause you to turn inwards and not relate at all. Venus leaves your sign and swims into your dreamy finance and value sector.

Friday 26th

Venus rules money so be very careful now as your hard-earned cash will be spent as soon as it's earned while she is here. If you insist on spending, make sure it's on something that nurtures you. Frivolous purchases may attract you, but you will regret them in the long run.

Saturday 27th

A bright Full Moon in your intimacy sector may show how you are hard on yourself and don't allow time to explore the deeper issues of life. Joint finances need to be checked now as there may be payments overdue or subscriptions that have expired.

Sunday 28th

The energy is very grounding today which may make you feel at odds. Being an air sign, you dislike being tied down. However, this time is best for administration work, checking finances and getting long-standing jobs done. When you see your 'to do' list diminish, you will be pleased.

MARCH

· · · · · · · · · · · · · · · · · ·

Monday 1st

Make use of today's energy to say what you need to the right people. You may have someone to impress now. There is a chance that you are also asking the right questions and gaining insight into what your self-improvement is all about this year, listen carefully to anyone acting as a guide or teacher.

Tuesday 2nd

Continue using your mental faculties to network with others and achieve balance and harmony in your mind. You may be learning about another culture and feel that this will fit well with your current way of thinking or enhance a new direction. Stretch yourself and broaden your horizons.

Wednesday 3rd

The Moon is in your career sector. Here is where you put everything you have into getting to the bottom of a problem. Be detective like now. Your outgoing personality can knuckle down and explore every level in the workplace. Be mindful that you need a good home-work balance.

Thursday 4th

Today can be a little tricky as you may come across objections to your point of view today. You may have worked hard on a project only to have it questioned by someone in authority and this will make your temper flare. Mars moves into your creative sector to help you get focused.

Friday 5th

The Moon moves into your social sector just in time for the weekend. Plans with your friends and wider groups will fill you with optimism. There will be much to talk about when Mercury meets Jupiter but be careful that you don't only talk about yourself.

Saturday 6th

You may be having a great time with your close friends today. Reminiscing and laughter will be the best remedy for a heavy week. You may be more emotionally invested than usual in paying long-distance visits so get out your planner and organise something for this year.

Sunday 7th

As the Moon dips into your hidden sector you may feel the need to have some alone time to recharge and get back into work mode. You must learn how to nurture yourself at these times. A connection to Venus helps you to be light-hearted and less serious. You may have some innovative ideas now.

Monday 8th

This is a great time to combine your long-term goals with your deepest desires. Begin to pull out and vocalise your dreams as this is the first step to manifesting them. Make sure that they are realistic and tangible, and you will not fail. Keep hold of what is important to you.

Tuesday 9th

The early hours may have you awake with troubling thoughts. Your erratic, spontaneous self feels too controlled right now. This isn't a bad thing; this is Pluto telling you that some things need to go to make room for your new growth.

Wednesday 10th

The Sun meets Neptune today and your future is staring you in the face. Is it real, you may ask? Neptune allows you to look at things from a different perspective and will give you more options. The Sun will burn away any fogginess and you will have more clarity on how to proceed.

Thursday 11th

While the Moon remains in your sign, concentrate on what you put out into the world versus how you really feel. Mercury meets the Moon and your heart and mind are in sync. However, the trick now is to put this into action and not try to keep up an outdated façade.

Friday 12th

A dreamy Moon in your finance sector warns against over-eating, overspending and being stubborn with this. Try to use this empathic energy to come up with a new quest for connection which actually leads somewhere. The retrogrades this summer will challenge you greatly in this regard.

Saturday 13th

Today there's a New Moon in your finance and values sector. This Moon also meets Neptune. This is a brilliant opportunity to make plans and goals regarding what treasure you hold and what new treasure you seek. Pluto is in the background asking that you release something first.

Sunday 14th

This is an especially dreamy day because Venus meets Neptune. This energy is so surreal that you may feel that you have drifted off to a fantasy island and wish to stay there. Look for the signposts that point to the real world and the wonderful journey ahead of you.

Monday 15th

You're filled with motivation now. You may find that your communications are like a hotline today and you just can't get enough done. Networking with others via email, messaging or phone will provide you with plenty of ideas which you will be eager to initiate.

Tuesday 16th

Your self-control is good today and you find that you're implementing new ways of thinking about past hurts. An uplifted mood goes with you in all that you do. This will mostly be seen in your family sector today where you are the multitasker, provider and nurturer of your household.

Wednesday 17th

Mercury has just flown into your finance sector. He can curb your spending and help you budget for things while here. Families may be unstable today and you may find yourself using a harsh tone in order to get the harmony back. Pushing people's buttons won't work.

Thursday 18th

Jupiter is now squaring off with the Moon and you may have a hard time laying the law down. Perhaps it's best that you let this slide as this tough energy will pass soon. You may be too used to getting your own way simply because you take on multiple roles.

Friday 19th

If you have a creative project or a romantic pursuit, today is a good day to do something about them. Mars sits with the Moon giving anything that you are passionate about a softer edge. You don't have to be forceful today. Things will flow easily. Use passion, not logic.

Saturday 20th

Today is the Spring Equinox. Day and night are equal lengths. The Sun is at the first point of the zodiac and you may feel a sense of anticipation. Try to stay still and patient and feel into this tension. When the time is right, you'll spring into action.

Sunday 21st

Venus becomes the warrior Goddess as she joins the Sun in your communication sector. You will find that any networking you need to do will be tempered with compassion. You need not be aggressive to get what you want now. Love will go a lot further than you realise.

Monday 22nd

Today you must see to the mundane jobs in your life. This may not be very interesting or raise your profile in the way you wish but it's vital. Take this opportunity to check in with your body and get some routine health checks. You may have some ingenious ideas today.

Tuesday 23rd

Your true north, as represented by Neptune, calls you today. There are plans you must put in place in order to follow this path to a higher version of yourself. Pluto in your hidden sector opposes the Moon and you may feel vulnerable and stubborn. Be gentle with yourself but make that shift now.

Wednesday 24th

The energy today may feel difficult to navigate. The Moon is in your relationship sector and you wish to parade with a loved one and be the centre of attention. However, Venus is in the heart of the Sun and is invisible. Leave the catwalk show for another time.

Thursday 25th

You may be very frustrated today. You want to be seen out and about, but this isn't possible. Be content with the closest company you have and enjoy them for who they are. Today is not about you. Stop sulking and let another shine for a change.

Friday 26th

This morning the Moon moves into your intimacy sector where you have a better chance of feeling important. You don't miss a trick here as you scrutinise everything you're told to the point of obsession. You may unearth something that's been hidden from you for a while.

Saturday 27th

Just as you think you're on top of things and order has been resumed, the Moon opposes Mercury and Neptune and you have brain-fog. Nothing is clear to you today. Don't try to persevere as you will become more muddled. Let this energy pass and try again tomorrow.

Sunday 28th

A Full Moon may show where you're out of balance in your relationship with the rest of the world. Perhaps you probe too deeply and have scared someone away. You may also be overthinking the simplest of things and cause more problems for yourself. What is the Moon showing you?

Monday 29th

Mars and Jupiter combine today to help you charge ahead with a love interest or a creative project. Jupiter loves it when things get big and bold and Mars is assertive and driven. Approach what you do today with vigour and intensity. This may be a lucky day for you.

Tuesday 30th

Mercury meets Neptune and together they discuss how your
true north will help in your self-improvement. You're being
asked to investigate deeper and not to be afraid of what you
find. This is for the long-term; for today you may have to
balance your home and work duties.

Wednesday 31st

Insight comes to you by way of the intense Moon in your
career sector. Your social status is important to you and
you now realise that the work you do on yourself is going
to raise your profile even higher. You're prepared to do the
hard work now.

APRIL

....

Thursday 1st

Friends may lift you up today and your social interactions could be fun. Your outgoing mood makes you happy to listen to different opinions and think about whether they may be good to explore for yourself. Higher education or short courses may be something to think about. You're ready for something new.

Friday 2nd

Mercury and Pluto are catching up and you may feel this in your decisions to let go of vague ideas and concepts. An action plan that's solid and structured is needed now. Your online groups can help with this. You may find a valuable learned friend amongst them who can guide you.

Saturday 3rd

Your mind wanders off into fantasy thinking and conflicts with the plans you need to implement. Stick with what comes from your heart today. You must learn how to value what you have and not put too much importance on what you may never gain.

Sunday 4th

The Moon drops into your hidden sector and you may feel like some alone time. Without the distractions of the outer world, you're more likely to think clearly and responsibly. This is when you get your best ideas which are more likely to work for you. Dream if you will but keep it realistic.

Monday 5th

Mercury has entered your high-powered communications sector. Things are about to get noisy or even nosey. Write everything down now as you'll have a lot to remember. Your self-control is good today and you may be more productive than usual. This is a positive day.

Tuesday 6th

The Moon is now in your sign and you may be smiling and cheerful with all. You may be prepared to go the extra mile if it suits the common good. Your creativity reaches a new level and you may be sharing what you do. Members of the opposite sex achieve results together.

Wednesday 7th

Your drive and energy are on top form today. People notice that you put everything you have into your creative or romantic pursuits. The Moon meets Jupiter and inflates your ego but in a good way. You are proud of what you do. Good for you.

Thursday 8th

You must watch where your money goes today as this is the time of the month when you may see it slip through your fingers. Family issues may seem a little odd, but something is clearly brewing and ready to share. This can be anything from a great idea to a lovely surprise.

Friday 9th

Notice how your energy drops today. You may find that you struggle to keep a clear head as you drift off too easily. This can make you tired or drained. A high level of interaction in your creative and romantic sectors will be difficult to grasp.

Saturday 10th

You go from being only half there to fully present overnight. Your weekend is likely to be filled with messages, visits and chores. Venus and Jupiter connect to help you stay upbeat and cheerful. There is nothing you like more than catching up with people so enjoy your full weekend.

Sunday 11th

The Moon meets Mercury today and your busy weekend gets even busier. You may meet up with an old friend or a sibling and spend most of the day gossiping or laughing together. You'll be in just the right frame of mind and heart to make the most of this energy.

Monday 12th

The energy continues to be super-charged as a New Moon enters your communications sector. You may resolve not to leave it too long to catch up with your dearest friends. As the Moon meets Venus there is nice feminine energy waiting for you to access and indulge yourself with something.

Tuesday 13th

You may need to bring that energy back inwards and centre it around your home and family today. There is much to be done regarding housekeeping or caring for your family. You may have a moment of genius when the Moon meets Uranus. This could also be some frustration occurring.

. . . .

Wednesday 14th

Venus spends her last day in your communications sector. Now is the time to check that you haven't left anything outstanding that needs urgent attention and care. This may also involve money matters. You may find it hard to deal with other people's problems today. You multi-task badly.

Thursday 15th

As Venus now shifts into your family sector, you'll notice that things become easier to deal with. You're quite the expert in this department anyway, but you will find more time for yourself. Today you may have a lot to say for yourself. Words of love can come pouring out.

Friday 16th

Wearing your heart on your sleeve may make you more vulnerable today. You choose to share something deep and it may not go the way you desire. Your ruler in your sign pulls you back and helps you remember your own personal boundaries. You are safe.

Saturday 17th

The Moon meets Mars and you're emotionally driven to get an answer or complete a project. Your interactions with others may be highly active and busy. However, you may need to guard yourself against others who wish to probe too deeply for your liking. Make changes you are comfortable with.

Sunday 18th

After being busy yesterday, Mercury is now silent. You should be the same and only listen today. A quiet day in your own company will help you find your inner voice and follow that. Make yourself unavailable to others today and do your own thing. One day won't hurt.

Monday 19th

The Sun and Mercury enter your family sector together. This will be a great month for making money, family gatherings or home DIY. Decorating and making your home beautiful will be easily done with Venus here too. Bring out your exotic side and add some cultural influences to your surroundings.

Tuesday 20th

You may turn to a lover or close friend today and put your familial duties to one side. A certain person will bring out your self-expression and help you to grab a bit of the limelight you crave. Together you may plan to change the world or at least act for a good cause.

Wednesday 21st

Be careful how you express yourself as it may cause upset within your family. You may be shouting about something unusual or taboo. Someone who you see as an elder or teacher will show their disapproval. You may end up in the doghouse.

Thursday 22nd

Having had your say, you quieten down and your sense of responsibility returns. You needed to let off steam but now you are back to making sure everything is in order and chaos is behind you. Mars adds urgency to a creative or love project. Act now or regret it later.

Friday 23rd

Venus meets Uranus today. The planet of love tempers the disruptive influence of Uranus so expect a nice surprise. You may have hit a nerve with your recent behaviour and people are apologising to you. Mars enters your health and duties sector. Start a new exercise regime.

Saturday 24th

Mercury also meets Uranus now. Be very careful about what comes out of your mouth as this energy can make you gossip or spill a secret. This evening you may be very tired and fed up with any drama around you. Retreat if you can't find a happy balance here.

Sunday 25th

You may be challenged about your role in the family today. This may even come from you wishing to reorganise your own input and free up time for yourself. Do this with the compassion of Venus and the communication skills of Mercury and you may find that you are supported.

Monday 26th

Whatever you choose to do today, will be done with great vigour. You may be aiming to balance up all your duties and free time. Alternatively, you may be trying to reconcile your need for a holiday or a working vacation. Either way, you will be like a dog with a bone.

Tuesday 27th

A Full Moon lights up your career sector. This is very tricky as it opposes your home sector and will show up everything that has been going on here. You may need to justify yourself to more than one area of your life. Your social status may be at risk.

Wednesday 28th

Pluto turns retrograde today. This is going to be a time where you feel that you're done with self-improvement only to find another layer exists for you to tear through. Stick with it, this is hard work but extremely important and beneficial. Time to get real again.

Thursday 29th

A sociable Moon asks that you turn to your wider groups and soul friends. You have many contacts in all walks of life, now is the time to call in some favours. Your ruler, Saturn is quite happy for you to get some help if you are prepared to work.

Friday 30th

The Sun meets Uranus making an explosive time in your family sector. This may manifest as an argument, someone being exposed, or an innovative solution being found. Whichever one it is, you will be emotionally attached to this and find it hard to let go come nightfall.

MAY

. . . .

Saturday 1st

As the Sun is still sitting with Uranus, use today to get inspired
and put your own personal stamp on your home environment.
Be creative and individual. You might solve a long-standing
problem or see something in a completely new way. A rebellious
streak might take over and you go on strike.

Sunday 2nd

Your imagination knows no bounds. The deepest parts of your
psyche are revealing themselves and you deal with them well.
Look at your habits and conditioning, you are now strong
enough to make positive changes here. Things are beginning
to shift for you.

Monday 3rd

The Moon in your sign brings you new confidence. Managing
your duties and self-care may be easier now. Saturn curbs your
urge to rebel and you settle down to your responsibilities.
Money is well spent today and will bring long-term benefits.
A dream is beginning to manifest right before your eyes.

Tuesday 4th

Mercury moves into your creative sector. You may find that
your self-expression is more eloquent and persuasive now. If
you have love to profess to someone special, do it now. This is
a good time for expression of all kinds so get out the thesaurus
and start writing. Love poetry will go down well.

Wednesday 5th

The Moon flies by Jupiter and gives your emotions a boost of joy. You might feel on top of the world today. It's possible that you drift off to a fantasy place and have trouble being logical, but this is fine. Work this energy to your advantage and be original.

Thursday 6th

Neptune hosts the Moon and you may have a pull towards a long-lost dream. This may involve some finances but will ultimately bring you some happiness in the home. You are taking the small steps needed to implement change and let go of old and worn habits or items.

Friday 7th

There's something important that you need to do regarding truth, travel or higher education. Jupiter is about to leave your sign and warns that you need to attend to this now. This is another easy day where change comes naturally. Plans can be put on paper.

Saturday 8th

Conversations are highly active today. Be careful that they don't get aggressive. You may have a very busy weekend with the Moon in your communications sector. Catching up with people will be fun as will chatting or messaging a lover or special friend. Leave time to unwind this evening.

Sunday 9th

Venus is now in your creative sector. She will add love, harmony and beauty to whatever you choose to make or do now. Love exchanges are highlighted and getting to know someone will be high on your agenda. A family gathering might end the weekend with good food and company.

Monday 10th

It's possible that you feel something bubbling up inside you. Mars makes a helpful connection to the Moon and helps you to get through your daily routine. By evening, you may either erupt with emotions or find an ingenious way to tackle an old problem.

Tuesday 11th

Today there's a New Moon in your family sector. If there's something you wish to begin, change or let go of, now is the time to put this in place. Discipline may be the issue and you may need to get all family members on board first. Work as a family unit.

Wednesday 12th

The Moon meets Venus and they send feminine, intuitive energy to your creative sector. This is a great day for romance. You can allow yourself to be vulnerable and share some of your innermost secrets with a person who you trust. This will release some pressure from you.

Thursday 13th

Your head and heart are in sync. You may be emotionally attached now and in the process of exploring boundaries with a new person. Jupiter has jumped into your finance and values sector. Luck and love have entered your life hand in hand. Time for meaningful connections with others.

. . . .

Friday 14th

It feels like you're on cloud nine. Your mind is full of racing thoughts, but you can't quite grasp them. Neptune is shrouding you with a mist and not giving you any clarity. This may serve to protect you from getting ahead of yourself. Wait until the energy shifts.

Saturday 15th

Your desire to be of service to people you feel strongly about is activated. Emotional energy from Jupiter and the Moon surrounds you. If you had a million dollars you would give it away now. Altruism is one of your strong points and it's certainly showing.

Sunday 16th

Passion drives you today. The Moon meets Mars and you could be in for a steamy night. A connection to Neptune and Uranus indicates that dreamy, floaty and earth-shattering activity is on the menu. Allow yourself to be vulnerable and you'll be protected by someone who cares about you.

Monday 17th

Pluto sits opposite the Moon and this may challenge you in ways you find difficult. How much control do you have? Do you need to let old habits die in order to enjoy this new opportunity? This might niggle you today. Think about it without dwelling on it too much.

Tuesday 18th

When the Moon is in your relationship sector you feel like stepping out and parading with your partner. Show off your status and take pride in each other without forcing it onto others. Remember that you're an individual and need not be defined by the partnerships you have.

Wednesday 19th

As the Moon shifts today, it opposes Jupiter. You may find that your ego is rather large right now but isn't doing you any favours. Ego can protect or project and today it may be projecting your image in a negative way. Check-in with yourself. Give yourself a pep talk.

Thursday 20th

You may have finally come down to earth and are processing recent events. Be careful not to over analyse things and set your wandering mind on an unnecessary journey. Venus and Saturn are connecting well to help you be respectful and responsible. Love yourself first, everyone else comes later.

Friday 21st

Today may be a good time to check on your health. You could have some brain fog so concentrate your efforts on grounding your body. Look at your diet and ensure that you're getting the exercise you need. You can't give if your own cup is half empty.

Saturday 22nd

Your ruler, Saturn, turns retrograde in your sign. This will bring a period of evaluating your responsibilities. You will need to pull back from external activities that have no real value to your daily life. Others will begin to see the real you shine through the façade you tend to wear.

Sunday 23rd

Today may be a balancing act between yourself and others. Look at how you lead and how you connect. Is there another avenue you would like to explore now? You may feel an aggressive urge to broaden your horizons or learn about other cultures. More change is coming.

Monday 24th

The week begins with an intense Moon in your career sector. It's possible that you need to put your nose to the grindstone or do some detective work. You may feel some jealousy towards colleagues and cause some upset. Your status may be challenged, and you take that home with you.

Tuesday 25th

The Moon makes a connection to newly retrograde Saturn. You may be called to do something which leaves a bad taste in your mouth. Someone has to do it, it may as well be you. However, you begrudge this and get emotional about it. Communications can be difficult today.

Wednesday 26th

A Full Moon occurs in your social sector. Friendships and acquaintances are under fire. You may realise that some contacts are not in your best interests. Let these go with love and compassion and learn to have better boundaries when meeting new people in the future.

Thursday 27th

A social event with people you trust and admire may be just the thing. Long-distance friendships may offer you more support than your geographically close ones. Indeed, you may be complaining about your local friends and wishing you were nearer the ones you find more interesting. You may be a little two-faced today.

Friday 28th

Mercury turns retrograde tomorrow so use today to do all the necessary preparation. Back up all your devices, double check travel plans and abstain from signing commitments if possible. Time alone is well spent today as Jupiter can help you be honest with yourself. A little self-talk will go a long way.

Saturday 29th

Mercury speaks to Venus as he turns retrograde. He leaves her to help you be kind, compassionate and harmonic in your artistic and romantic ventures. You are ready for this retrograde and your self-control is on top form. Cautiously but confidently, you step into the outside world.

Sunday 30th

Relax. The Moon has dropped into your sign and you feel fully alert and outgoing. There is no need to put on a show because you are being your natural self and people are loving it. You can charm everyone you meet today with your light-hearted, optimistic outlook on life.

Monday 31st

Saturn and the Moon meet up. You may feel this acutely as all eyes are on you. You may be overly worried about messing up in front of an audience. However, you may be more articulate, driven and passionate than you have been for some time. Start as you mean to go on.

JUNE

. . . .

Tuesday 1st

As the Sun joins the point of fate, you may catch a glimpse of your distant future. There may be more than one possibility to choose from. The Moon meets Jupiter in your sign and gives you the thumbs up. Whichever path you choose will be right for you.

Wednesday 2nd

Indecision still bothers you. If you find yourself being whimsical and non-committal, take time out and connect to your spirit. Venus enters your health and duties sector where she will teach you more about giving unconditionally. Your intuition and nurturing skills will become finely tuned now. Use this energy wisely.

Thursday 3rd

Today you get another look at the future you should be building for yourself. The Moon hangs around with Neptune, who acts as your inner compass. Follow your heart and keep all rational thinking out of it. That will become useful once you have aligned yourself to your path.

Friday 4th

You wish to speak to as many people as you can who can help you on your path. Your mind may be overloaded with well-meaning information and it's down to you to filter through it. You may need to step aside and come back to this at a later date.

Saturday 5th

There's very tricky energy for you to navigate. Your heart and mind are in discussions, but you feel defensive and unwilling to give anything up in favour of possibilities. Throw caution to the winds and step into the unknown, it will be an adventure.

Sunday 6th

This morning you seek solace in the comfort of family. You may be hosting a dinner or simply doing all your chores with a smile. Home life with your nearest and dearest will suit you well enough today. Lucky Jupiter and caring Venus are on your side, helping to move things along.

Monday 7th

The Moon pays her monthly visit to Uranus. At these times your emotions may be unstable, or you come up with innovative and unusual ideas. Saturn makes this a challenging day but be sure to look out for the lesson and not focus on the hardship.

Tuesday 8th

Today is best spent doing grounding activities. You may choose to cook and eat, exercise or walk in nature. You will probably do whatever you choose, to excess, but don't worry, an evening spent taking care of yourself will ease the pain. Are you reinventing yourself again?

Wednesday 9th

The Moon now meets the point of fate and this is more marked as it follows the Sun. Your emotions may swing one way and then the other but try to harness this wild energy. Get creative and write about it. Saturn is watching and assessing how you deal with uncertainty now. He will enjoy seeing you productive.

Thursday 10th

A New Moon in your creative sector meets Mercury retrograde.
Don't make any commitments today. If you have any ideas
or intentions, note them and wait until Mercury turns direct
before acting on them. Your thoughts may not be clear today
so play it safe and wait until the energy shifts.

Friday 11th

Mercury is silent today. You must be on the lookout for
messages, symbols and dreams from him. These will be like
signposts you should follow after his retrograde. Mars enters
your relationship sector to heat things up a little. Things may
get passionate or argumentative while he's here.

Saturday 12th

Use the day to get in touch with the lovely feminine energy
provided by the Moon and Venus. Mothers and female relatives
will feature heavily. Women's wisdom will guide and nourish
you. This is just the day to nurture your inner child and feel
maternal love surrounding you.

Sunday 13th

Today may feel challenging as you wish to break free from
confinement and run free. You're called to Neptune's fantasy
island. This is an attempt on your part to avoid dealing with an
unsavoury situation. Face it, there can be no growth without
some pain. This is for your own good.

Monday 14th

Your mood may be close to boiling point today. It's possible that
you've gone against the words of authority or an elder and been
reprimanded. Uranus, the disruptive planet, sticks his nose in
and tempers may flare. Saturn isn't very pleased with you today.

Tuesday 15th

Your recent mood may have affected time with a lover or close friend. This may be down to Mercury but is also down to your stubborn refusal to change your ways at times. Look at what triggered this and vow to work on it slowly. Saturn and Uranus are waiting for more trouble.

Wednesday 16th

This morning you come back to normality and make amends. You dislike chaos and bad atmospheres and tend to gloss over them rather than work on them. However, today you may have a mind to put things right before moving on. Harmony is restored by being grounded and rational.

Thursday 17th

There's still a danger lurking as the Moon and Mercury square off. If you prefer to keep the peace, then say nothing today. Be present but humble. Women can help you get back to a state of inner peace. Avoid impulse buys and quick fixes as they won't do you any good.

Friday 18th

Helpful connections to Mars and Pluto restore balance. You may breathe a little easier. Your mind is turned outwards and you're more inclined to see another point of view. Relationships will benefit from you being more gracious and less selfish. Work on this.

Saturday 19th

You know that you should be grateful for the people in your life who put you back on the right track. Making another person feel special as a way of saying thank you, will be remembered in the future. Try being the nurturer instead of the needy today.

Sunday 20th

Jupiter is about to turn retrograde. He will retreat into your sign and help Saturn level up your lessons this year. You may be tossed and turned but, like laundry, you'll come out of it clean and fresh. Accept the ebb and flow and learn to be more adaptable with yourself.

Monday 21st

The Summer Solstice sees the Sun enter your health and duties sector. The longest day is a time to look back on your achievements so far this year. Take a deep breath and expel gratitude for this. Take another and ask for guidance to survive the retrograde period in your sign.

Tuesday 22nd

Mercury turns direct. Any creative or romantic pursuits that have been affected by his retrograde now have to chance to be revived. An outgoing Moon in your social sector asks if you have time for a social event. This will help you let off steam safely with friends.

Wednesday 23rd

You may be in a sociable mood but watch that your reckless attitude doesn't catch you out today. There is a tendency to be too much for some people or you may have triggers that touch on sore parts of your psyche. Tread carefully and stay gentle and light-hearted.

Thursday 24th

A Full Moon lights up your deepest, darkest parts. You risk exposing inner wounds that have not yet healed. If you're not ready for this process, use the Full Moon energy to look around by yourself. You may be surprised to see what you have already healed this year.

Friday 25th

Neptune turns retrograde. You must be very careful with money now. Ethereal ideas will attract you, but you soon realise that you've wandered down a one-way street as they have no substance. Use this retrograde to learn what has true value and what is an illusion.

Saturday 26th

You may have a sleepless night and wake to feeling vulnerable or let down. Planetary energy is difficult to deal with today. As it's the weekend, why not take a day off and hide under the duvet with a good book? You will not want to be sociable now.

Sunday 27th

The Moon in your sign is still making you uncomfortable.
The heavy retrograde energy may be affecting your sense of
self. This will pass and you will stabilise again soon. Venus
moves into your relationship sector. Love, beauty and harmony
will enhance your most important interactions. Partners can
be relied on now.

Monday 28th

Jupiter exaggerates the mood you are in today. Remember
that he is retrograde and is waiting for you to realize what
this lesson will be. He likes truth, justice, joy and optimism so
work on those themes regarding your self-image. You desire to
connect on a spiritual level now.

Tuesday 29th

A dreamy Moon makes you extra-emotional. You may desire to
pull all your dearest friends and relatives around you and hug
them all. You may just have to make do with sending messages
or making phone calls and checking in with loved ones. They
will appreciate this very much.

Wednesday 30th

The Moon meets newly retrograde Neptune. This may feel
confusing at first until you see that patience is needed. As
your inner compass, it may feel broken or misaligned, but the
lesson today is patience. You may also learn to look at things
from a different perspective. Well done.

JULY

. . . .

Thursday 1st

Communications might be strained today. There may be a
tendency to be over-assertive or aggressive with your closest
partnerships. Being stubborn or reluctant to go along with
the plans of another may cause problems. Make sure that
you're clear and concise, and no misunderstandings occur.
Be compassionate and mindful of other's feelings.

Friday 2nd

This is a better day to get your point across. Mercury helps you
to express yourself and to see different points of view. You may
temper that aggression with passion, and this can give you a
better connection to your partner. If personal boundaries are
respected, then you can achieve harmony.

Saturday 3rd

A weekend at home may be the answer to the frustrations you
have been experiencing. You may want to switch things up
with a home make-over or a clear out. You will soon notice the
space you're making for something more worthwhile to enter
your life.

Sunday 4th

Be careful that you're not overdoing change, as this may lead
you to feel uncomfortable again. It's possible that you're so
focused on your home and family that your love life will suffer
this weekend. The Moon has met Uranus and you might feel
edgy and irritable.

Monday 5th

The week begins with a feeling of satisfaction. You see a way to reach your dreams and what needs to be tweaked in order to move forward. This will depend on how much you're willing to be humble and serve others. Home life continues to be important to you.

Tuesday 6th

Your creativity is highlighted now. The familiar itch you get when trying to initiate new projects comes to you. Your driving force needs to produce something beautiful, even if that's a simple conversation with a loved one. You may have a battle of head and heart. Sit with this and process it.

Wednesday 7th

Venus is in the spotlight today in your relationship sector. Today will be all about how you achieve harmony. You may find that selfish feelings surface as Venus opposes your ruler. This is asking you to stop and consider what's triggering you as it may be an outdated habit.

Thursday 8th

The Moon meets Mercury and your head may be filled with ideas and concepts that are hard to express. As they are in your creative sector, use this energy to produce some of your best work. A poem, piece of music or a good conversation may help you untangle your thoughts and feelings.

. . . .

Friday 9th

You feel duty-bound and are happy to see to the mundane jobs and chores you need to do. This is a nurturing aspect for you and your caring instincts are activated. Work done now will be compassionate and touched with intuition and genius.

Saturday 10th

A New Moon in your health and duties sector gives you the chance to organise your schedule and prioritise your duties. Look at what you value the most and what gives you pleasure. This will likely trigger feelings of guilt or shame for putting yourself first too much. Work on this.

Sunday 11th

This is a day for love and romance as the young Moon enters your relationship sector. Saturn is opposite and is testing what you do now. Unselfish behaviour and total respect for your partner is needed. You can have a passionate time if you allow another to shine.

Monday 12th

Mars and Venus are dancing together. The Moon meets them both and emotions are high. You may feel something bubbling under the surface and worry a little. No need to fear, this is love and passion making you vulnerable. Remain open for your nearest and dearest.

Tuesday 13th

Mars and Venus have met. This can be fireworks for you. The celestial lovers ask that you combine masculine and feminine in the best of ways now. Your energy and drive will be in line with your need for passion and harmony. Stay open to exciting possibilities with your lover.

Wednesday 14th

Two hearts and minds can unite or start a war. Your intimacy sector hosts the Moon while Mars and Venus are still loved up. How deeply do you wish to relate? If you're uncertain, talk about this and get very clear on your own personal boundaries.

Thursday 15th

Neptune is getting your attention. Remember that he's retrograde and confusing you a little. The prize is being dangled before your eyes, but you're unable to grasp it. Note it, for now, keep it in your mind and reach again when the energy is better, and you have more clarity.

Friday 16th

Today your yearning for bigger and better things may take you to associates in distant lands. Your sense of satisfaction never lasts long enough, and you're always looking for more. You must learn how to balance what you have with what you may or may not achieve.

Saturday 17th

The weekend brings you back to love and romance. You look to your relationships to reconcile your need for more. You may now realise how important these relationships are. Pluto is nagging you to transform old ideas and coping mechanisms about safety and security. They may have worked once, but not now.

Sunday 18th

An intense Moon in your career sector causes you to put your energy into work today. You may need to spend time looking at taxes or shared accounts. Mercury helps you to make decisions about this which may be uncomfortable for some. Be careful, you may have to upset someone.

Monday 19th

You are highly driven and almost ruthless. Money matters may come to a head and need to be dealt with once and for all. You may find that money is one of your deeply hidden issues and times like this force you to deal with it.

Tuesday 20th

You're outgoing and wish to connect with friends and associates from your wider groups. This may be good for you as you're more open to learning from experienced friends now. A teacher may cross your path and offer some wisdom. You may also talk too much today.

Wednesday 21st

Chatting with a lover or close friend will lift you up and make you more optimistic. Do your visions match? Are your wider interests similar? You may find that conversations that happen today can put you both in the spotlight and make you feel untouchable when together.

Thursday 22nd

Venus moves into your intimacy sector. How deep is your love? You'll be getting to know someone on a different level now. The Sun heats things up in your relationship sector now too. This is an optimum time for love and romance. Step up and step out together.

Friday 23rd

The Moon meets Pluto in your hidden sector. You will feel
stirrings which are telling you to get rid of old baggage.
Neptune beckons and you now know that the release of the
old will help you get back aligned with your inner compass,
although be prepared as this may take some time.

Saturday 24th

There's a bright Full Moon in your sign. This will show you
how much you've already worked on yourself and what has
worked for you. Have a talk with yourself and give yourself
some credit. Mercury hears your pep talk and puts you a little
closer to your true north.

Sunday 25th

You may feel agitation as the Moon connects to both Mars and
Uranus. Know that this is your defence mechanism kicking in
and that you've defaulted to old ways of protecting yourself.
Mercury opposes Pluto and reminds you of your progress so
far. Keep working on this.

Monday 26th

Today can be tricky and your self-worth comes under fire. You
may be feeling useless or disappointed with yourself. Kicking
yourself won't help. Make a note of what has triggered you
recently and resolve to go easy on yourself. You're not going to
change overnight.

. . . .

Tuesday 27th

The Moon meets Neptune and you may feel dreamy and floaty. Try not to let yourself be drawn into unrealistic thinking. You may see spiritual paths as the answer to everything, but the work you need to do is more grounded than that. Stay real and sensible now.

Wednesday 28th

Jupiter returns to your sign as if to tell you that if you mess up now, it will be huge. This isn't the time for rebellious outbreaks. You must listen to the wise, pay attention to your elders and stay on the right side of the law. Take extra care with others now.

Thursday 29th

You must look before you leap. You may have an urge to be outrageous and express your individuality, but this will do you no favours. Everything must be done by the book today. Check the manual, know your rights and scan every detail before doing something.

Friday 30th

Start to wind down for a weekend by doing homely activities with your clan. Plans can be made which involve restoration projects or home makeovers. Your family may notice a shift in you and find you difficult to deal with. This says more about them than you. You are transforming, remember that.

Saturday 31st

The grounded Moon may make you appear stubborn and wilful. You may have cross words with a lover and be unwilling to see another's point of view. This may be a day better spent by baking, decorating and tantalising your senses. Doing your own thing won't hurt for one day.

AUGUST

. . . .

Sunday 1st

Home life can be stressful today. You may wish to escape and
be with your lover instead. There may be too much going on
for you to think clearly. Use this time with Mercury in the
heart of the Sun to be silent and ignore the noise around you.

Monday 2nd

Conflicts can arise and you may find that you're unable
to do your own thing. This is teaching you the art of
compromise. You may feel resentful to those who take up
your time and have a tantrum about it. Try another way of
expressing yourself.

Tuesday 3rd

You may be wistful and wish to reach out and engage with
something different. Your thoughts are busy, but you're
unable to settle on one thing. You have a niggling feeling that
something may be missing from your life. Your lover may have
some answers for you.

Wednesday 4th

You're out of sorts and not sure why. Neptune evades you when
you try to anchor yourself and your true north seems out of
reach again. Family life conflicts with your love life today and
things may get out of hand. Take some time alone this evening
to nurture yourself.

Thursday 5th

The energy today makes you much calmer. You could be spoiling yourself with self-care or simply enjoying some favourite foods. Getting deep into a good book will also help. You may wish to think about getting health checks now as they may be overdue. Alone time will help you restore inner peace.

Friday 6th

You may be on the receiving edge of other's impatience as they need you to return to your role in the family or your relationship. Remind them that you are self-nurturing and will be back on top form soon enough. They need to allow you some time for yourself.

Saturday 7th

You're ready to step up and share your fire. Your return to outside life is bold and colourful. This shows your ability to bounce back after time out. This may cause some friction in the family, but the spotlight is clearly on you and your needs right now.

Sunday 8th

A New Moon in your relationship sector allows you to make new resolutions regarding how you relate and partner in your life. Saturn, your ruler, sits opposite and clues you up on what to wish for. There must be a balance between you and others from now on.

Monday 9th

As the Moon passes by Mercury, talks with a loved one can be fruitful and understanding. A shift in focus to your intimacy sector aids in cleaning out unnecessary and superficial complaints. You may now focus on real issues and dismiss petty arguments. Service to others is commendable and mutual now.

Tuesday 10th

Your emotions may confuse you but as this is only a passing phase don't worry too much. The Moon meets Mars and you have the energy to deal with money or deep issues. This may drain you if you take it too seriously. Venus opposing Neptune also emphasises the need to hold on to your cash today.

Wednesday 11th

You may now feel some of the changes you have been making subconsciously. The Moon meets Venus and they have a heart to heart about self-care and needless worries. Things are not as big as they seem. Your ability to deal with these triggers is improving.

Thursday 12th

Mercury has entered your intimacy sector and you may find that the trickier concepts of life interest you more. You may be more inquisitive and ready to learn than usual. You're balanced and accepting of change now that you have experienced its worth. Well done.

Friday 13th

You can wear as many masks as you like but the one that people will be attracted to is the authentic you. You wear your heart on your sleeve and nothing is hidden. Your charm and individuality will go a long way today. Just be yourself, no need to act.

Saturday 14th

The weekend sees an intense Moon in your career sector. Don't make yourself a weekend worker without reaping any benefits. Your drive is to please others but Saturn watches how you momentarily forget about self-care. Enjoy some time to relax over the weekend or lose that time altogether.

Sunday 15th

You may be frustrated as money issues arise for you to deal with. There may some jealousy or unrealistic ideas about how to advance in the workplace. Your social status is important but can wait until the weekend is over. Have some downtime or you'll regret it later.

Monday 16th

If you're not careful, you may get involved in petty squabbles which can turn nasty. Thankfully Venus enters your travel sector and can help to smooth things over by messaging, emails or other means of communication. This is another lesson on boundaries and self-worth and Saturn is watching once more.

Tuesday 17th

You're outgoing today and wish to share your optimism with your wider groups. Learning something new may be useful in the future so hold on to it and look at other educational possibilities. You may now see the futility of some of your dreams and visions.

Wednesday 18th

You become more serious and withdrawn. Emotionally, you may feel like a roller coaster but go with the flow and for now that flow asks you to come down to earth. This is the time to process recent events and new situations. Take your time to ensure that you've understood.

Thursday 19th

Uranus, the disruptive planet, turns retrograde. This will affect your family life so prepare for some rebellious acts and surprises. Mercury and Mars meet up making your words heated. This combination can be argumentative or ingenious. You may unearth more pearls from your psyche ready for healing.

Friday 20th

This can be a tricky day to navigate if you try to do too much. The Moon meets Pluto who is checking in with your self-improvement. You may feel like this work is never-ending, but you are a deep, old soul and there's much to discover. Be gentle with yourself.

Saturday 21st

There are many rumblings going on in your family sector and these are causing you deep distress. If you must lay the law down and take responsibility, then do so. There may not be anyone else who can take the role. Be adult and compassionate as you do so.

Sunday 22nd

There's a Full Moon in your sign. You may feel exposed and naked today as all eyes are on you. Take this as a compliment, you're showcasing the important work of this year. The Sun moves into your intimacy sector to highlight the pearls within.

Monday 23rd

Be very careful with money. The Moon is in your dreamy finance and values sector and you may not have a good grip on your cash. It could slip away easily so only spend on what is necessary. You may need to fight off the demons enticing you to make a large purchase.

Tuesday 24th

As the Moon meets Neptune, you see your true north as if through a misty lens. It's there but not attainable today. You may have a talk with yourself and take notes for when you have more clarity. Mercury wants to hear your thoughts now, share them with a close friend or lover.

Wednesday 25th

Mercury sits opposite Neptune and together they talk in an unknown language. You won't get much done today and may even experience a headache or brain-fog. You're so out of balance that you may need to take a day off and rest.

Thursday 26th

Communications of all sorts may be hard to manage. There is a need to initiate projects and do some research, but the energy is preventing you from thinking straight. If you try, you'll get in a muddle. Continue to rest and do mundane things instead.

Friday 27th

The Moon is back in your family sector and you may get some respite from taking things slowly and seeing to household chores. This may not gel with your sense of individuality but will help you to regroup and remember that your family is your team and they are all rooting for you.

Saturday 28th

The Moon meets newly retrograde Uranus. This may be unsettling or productive. It will show you more about the changes needed in your life. You may be surprised at how this is not as huge as you think. Others will rally round if you have suggestions for improving family life.

Sunday 29th

Enjoy time with your nearest and dearest today as the planetary energy is supportive. You may find that a family conference is more productive than you hoped. Good communication between members will show that all are aware of positive change and how this can be implemented.

Monday 30th

The Moon in your creative sector helps you to express your wishes clearly. They are received well by others and a plan is put into action. Mercury flies into your travel sector to help with long-distance communication and higher education. What do you wish to learn about?

Tuesday 31st

You may feel a little tense. You momentarily panic and believe that you've lost sight of your true north for good. This isn't true. This is a passing phase and will be all right again in the morning. No need to panic and worry. Breath easily and relax.

SEPTEMBER

. . . .

Wednesday 1st

You must look after your own health and wellbeing. That little voice inside you will try to make you feel guilty for doing so, but don't listen. Take some time out and cook your favourite foods, be with your special people and read a good book. Make the most of 'you' time.

Thursday 2nd

Surprise yourself today or buy yourself a treat. Listen to your intuition to tell you how to care for yourself. You may have a long list of things to do but ignore them. Mars opposing Neptune demands that you make time in your schedule for more times like this.

Friday 3rd

If you have managed to refresh your energy levels and not feel manipulated by others, you may enjoy partner time this evening. Go with the flow again today and be guided by your instincts and own needs. You will be rewarded with better mental health.

Saturday 4th

A fiery Moon lifts your spirits and energy and you may find balance in reaching out to others who are from a different culture. Broaden your horizons today but stay safe with online interactions. Your desire to connect may lead you astray and personal boundaries may be violated. Be brave but cautious.

Sunday 5th

The weekend continues with the Moon in your relationship sector. A good connection to harmonising Venus helps you share that Aquarius love. An opposition to Jupiter may see you struggle with leaders or fail to see a broader point of view. This may make you rebellious and defiant.

Monday 6th

Pluto is bringing things up again for you to transform or discard. This is all part of your healing process and you will feel empowered when it's done. Your instinct to connect with all may put these plans in jeopardy so be sure that your interactions with others are safe and responsible.

Tuesday 7th

Today there is a tricky New Moon in your intimacy sector. You may find that you wish to be more helpful and less selfish with your deepest connections. Learn humility and resolve to be very clear with new friendships. Your energy is high, but you may suffer from over-exertion today.

Wednesday 8th

Look at how you relate to others from different backgrounds. Are you accepting or excepting? Do you exclude others if they don't have the same life experiences as you? Saturn is pleased as you take on board all manners of safe and responsible connecting.

Thursday 9th

Your head and heart are in sync. A head full of chatter is a happy head as you're refining the way you communicate and relate. Mercury helps you to actively listen to others and offer useful information in return. This is a day of teaching and learning from others who differ greatly from you.

Friday 10th

Venus and the Moon both enter your career sector today. This wise feminine energy is useful for making your voice count in the workplace. Venus can be seductive here so don't be surprised if you are suddenly getting everything you want. Maybe now is the time to ask for a raise.

Saturday 11th

Work and home duties may clash, and you can't find the time to do it all. You may need to delegate or leave some chores for another time. If someone rattles you, try not to erupt in their face. The Moon's energy is somewhat blunt today.

Sunday 12th

Selfishness may cause a conflict. Be mindful that you don't upset a leader or person in authority. Emotions will be larger than usual and simple things can get out of hand. Your social circle calls this evening and you may be able to let off steam in a safe place.

Monday 13th

You're very talkative today. Your wider social groups are getting all your rants, ideas, plans and secrets. Make sure that you don't give away too much. Neptune calls but is teasing you again. You may be full of your dreams and visions but get belittled by someone.

Tuesday 14th

Good news! The Sun opposes Neptune and burns away all the mist helping you to see your true north very clearly. This gives you back your confidence and you're joyful and optimistic again. There's a chance that you get pushy today, but seductive Venus wins you over.

Wednesday 15th

The Moon is in your hidden sector and you're able to process recent events and feelings. Isolation may do you some good today. Mars enters your travel sector and has itchy feet. You may be planning a trip that brings you closer to distant friends or lovers.

Thursday 16th

This is a great day for your work in progress. This morning you may be eager to go on an adventure or re-align yourself with your inner compass. The Moon meets Pluto and you feel the shift of transformation within you. Later, the Moon lands in your sign.

Friday 17th

The Sun makes a helpful connection to Pluto and you know that you're on the right track with your inner work. However, fleeting connections from the Moon can make you irritable and impatient. Let these pass and focus on the deeper truths you have learned recently.

Saturday 18th

Enjoy simply being your unique self. The Moon meets Jupiter and you may find that you have aligned with a lawful or spiritual path you have been searching for. You now feel the urge to merge. Spiritual or unusual people call you to your higher and best self.

Sunday 19th

You may surprise yourself. Uranus in retrograde acts as a liberator for you. As Uranus co-rules your sign you may feel this as your call to adventure. You've ignored this for so long but this retrograde is giving you messages that are too strong to keep avoiding. Go for it.

Monday 20th

A beautiful Full Moon in your finance and value sector throws the spotlight over your own self-worth. You now wish to know your part in the collective is small but significant. Your inner compass is pointing to your true north. You must act on this today.

Tuesday 21st

Your mind is packed full of possibilities, enquiries and plans. It may be difficult to know where to start so ask for advice. Share your ideas. Be careful that you don't alienate those who can help you most by being too pushy. Be excited and driven but not aggressive, or else you may frighten people away.

Wednesday 22nd

The Autumn Equinox occurs tonight as the Sun enters your travel sector. Use this energy to pause and give gratitude for the long days of summer. The darker days will make you turn inwards and will enable you to consolidate your plans for adventure and transformation.

Thursday 23rd

You may be contemplating your immediate needs and your long-term needs. This will almost certainly be about how you relate and communicate with others. Giving and taking will be an issue today. Look towards your home and work lives for a compromise. You may need to merge these somehow.

Friday 24th

You may be reluctant to see to family duties today. Multi-tasking can be tedious or time-consuming. You have things you want to do for yourself but are called upon for your role as caregiver and homemaker. Resentment will build unless you resign yourself to these tasks.

Saturday 25th

Mercury turns retrograde tomorrow so use today to make all the necessary preparations. Back up all your devices and double-check travel plans. This retrograde will take place in your travel sector, so it is imperative that you drive safely and make solid arrangements when using transport. Road rage may be an issue now too.

Sunday 26th

Mercury retrograde begins. Meanwhile, the Moon is busy pulling the tides of your emotions. You may feel like you're drifting away from yourself and into unknown waters. Stay grounded and put an anchor out if you feel unsafe. This journey will only last the day.

Monday 27th

You may be in two minds today about a creative project or a love interest. Due to the Moon being in Mercury's sign, you would be better off waiting until the retrograde is over before putting paint on paper or professing undying love for someone. Be very cautious with self-expression now.

Tuesday 28th

If it's possible, take a day off and hide under your blankets. If there are any mishaps to be had from Mercury, today is the day they will occur. Late afternoon you may wish to take comfort in a nurturing environment. Women and mother figures are the ones to seek now.

Wednesday 29th

Someone may coax you out of your comfort zone. You may feel challenged and vulnerable. This can make you sulk like a small child and you may be prone to a tantrum. Venus and Neptune combine to make you seduced by fantasy thinking. You may be hard to deal with.

Thursday 30th

If you notice that your emotions are all over the place, flow with them. You may find something new to fix your wishful thinking on. This may be harmless but can also mean that you become so out of touch that you have difficulty coming back to earth.

OCTOBER

. . . .

Friday 1st

Partner time can help to chase the blues away. You may be
stubborn and resist any inner work presented to you because
today is all about how you are seen. You desire to get out and
be loud and visible. Let yourself go for one night only.

Saturday 2nd

Family duties may have to be put on hold today and this may
cause friction. You may not realise it, but things are shifting
naturally now. Your career is highlighted and gives you more
joy. This may be what was needed to change. Free up more
time for fun in the future.

Sunday 3rd

A quiet Sunday is needed in order to prepare for the coming
week. You may have to get deep into your accounts or do some
cleaning. Mercury may give you big problems today which
can affect your happy mood. If you feel stuck, take a break and
return with fresh eyes.

Monday 4th

Try to refrain from making an impulse buy today. Get serious
and not frivolous. Your bank balance may not support a major
purchase right now. If you're pining after something you desire,
make a list of the pros and cons involved and give yourself a
reality check.

Tuesday 5th

You may be more grounded today and accept that hard work is necessary before you reap any rewards. You have the ability to get to the bottom of something deep and your detective-like vigilance will be noted by those above you. Persuasion is your greatest ally so use it.

Wednesday 6th

A New Moon occurs in your travel sector. This Moon meets Mars and makes you driven to set goals and intentions regarding long-distance travel and higher education. Pluto turns direct and you may feel the shift as a lightening of your load. Constantly reinventing yourself is exhausting you.

Thursday 7th

It's possible that you feel some tension as the Moon squares off with newly direct Pluto. You may feel an emotional pull towards all that you have let go of this year, including part of your old identity. Venus glides into your social sector. Watch the invitations flood in now.

Friday 8th

The Sun and Mars are having a prolonged meet in your travel sector. This powerhouse of energy is ripe for you to commence your New Moon intentions. You may need to be strict with yourself and upset some family members but stick to your guns, the only way is up.

Saturday 9th

Today's energy can weigh heavy on you. Mercury joins the Sun and Mars and you may experience confusion, doubt and a relapse of your resolve. This will pass so distract yourself with quality time with your friends. Online associates can also help alleviate the stress you feel today.

Sunday 10th

Your ruler, Saturn, turns direct today. Your mood changes and you're more uplifted and hopeful. You seem to have broken through the brain-fog caused by Mercury and have your ego and drive back on track. Put your best foot forward now and implement your intentions.

Monday 11th

The week begins with the Moon still hanging about in your social sector, maybe you didn't have time to connect with everyone at the weekend and are still catching up. A person you admire gets your attention and time is well spent listening to their tales. Winding down this evening should be easy.

Tuesday 12th

Today you may stir something up in your family sector. This will ultimately be beneficial to your inner work. Something from the past may come up to be reviewed and healed. There may even be an unexpected surprise connected with a revelation. You may do a regular chore in a different way.

Wednesday 13th

The Moon meets newly direct Pluto. Take some time to listen to your inner voice and the praise it is giving you. Change is always difficult, but you have mastered that while Pluto has been in your hidden sector. You are permitted to see how your dreams might manifest.

Thursday 14th

In your sign, the Moon meets Saturn. Your wise but harsh teacher rewards you for the inner work you've done this year. Responsibilities don't have to be dull. Selfishness is not pretty. Personal boundaries are paramount. Well done for learning something new and accepting it as truth.

Friday 15th

Jupiter is giving you one last lesson before he too turns direct. What have you learned about truth, law, joy, and broadening your horizons whilst he has been in your sign? Take one last look around and ensure that your unique personality has uplifted those around you and benefited all.

Saturday 16th

You may enjoy a dreamy day today and follow your heart. There may be reminders of past losses and achievements, but you will also see future plans and how to develop them. Take a day of doing nothing except merging with things and people that you value highly.

Sunday 17th

Jupiter is now direct and will continue his journey through your sign. You may now step up your game and bounce happily through life knowing you are supported. When the Moon meets Neptune, you feel totally aligned with your true north and appreciate the process you have gone through this year.

Monday 18th

Mercury also turns direct now. You may make travel arrangements and review contracts or commitments you may have put on hold. Your communications sector will be buzzing with life. Write everything down in your planner and get ready to be the life and soul of upcoming parties.

Tuesday 19th

The Moon and Mercury are opposing each other, and you have a lot of information to sift through. Prioritise these and give yourself time to plan thoroughly. Mars and Jupiter combine to help you make long-distance travel a real possibility. Other cultures call you, as does higher education. Your social life is taking off.

Wednesday 20th

You may feel the strain of recent activity today. Mars energy is being drained by the opposing Full Moon in your communications sector. It's likely that a project has come to fruition and needs your full attention. There may be something to celebrate today. Go easy on yourself.

Thursday 21st

The Moon is now in your family sector and meets Uranus. This can be a volatile time as usual and you may need extra help around the house. Don't try doing it all alone as there's a chance of burn-out. Ask others to help you do the mundane chores.

Friday 22nd

Mars is squaring off with Pluto which may cause you to hide and isolate yourself. Think of it as self-preservation. You have to submit to time off if you need to keep energy for the things you enjoy most. Earthy grounded activities will help you stay focused and on task.

Saturday 23rd

The Sun enters your career sector and will aid in problem-solving. It will also highlight some nastiness or gossip in and around the workplace. You may experience jealousy as people may resent your climb to the top of the corporate ladder. Express yourself carefully with certain people.

Sunday 24th

There's a high chance that you speak out of turn today and upset someone from your social circle. Discord worries you and you should aim to put this right at the earliest opportunity. It may not be as serious as you think. You've simply said the wrong thing to the wrong person.

Monday 25th

You have an urge to take some steps towards your true north. Your path in life is right before your eyes and you must step forward bravely. Jupiter and Mars can help you to be courageous and remain optimistic about this. Don't let Neptune fool you.

Tuesday 26th

Your social circle may be casting doubts about your new ventures. This may be someone who's jealous of your trust in the universe and wishes they had the same opportunity. Be kind and compassionate to them. Tell them your story and they may begin to write their own.

Wednesday 27th

You may be exhausted by your mundane duties. Self-care is important. Neptune is still causing confusion and you may feel some doubt. Nurture yourself back to good mental health and you'll see that this was just a passing phase that you felt because you were in the flow.

Thursday 28th

If you feel drained, ask a partner to lift you up and take the lead. You'll feed off the attentive and vibrant personality and this will be enough to restore your normal easy-going nature. There's a party animal inside you just waiting to get out.

Friday 29th

Family and partners may both be requiring your presence today. This might be difficult to manage, and you'll need to do what's best for you, not them. Mercury lends you the gift of the gab and you can persuade others to do your bidding. People will fall in line once they know your feelings.

Saturday 30th

Mars enters your career sector with great force. With his help, you can storm through your daily work and complete project after project. This can also be a decluttering process where you review your work duties and ascertain whether they're really worth your effort.

Sunday 31st

Today you think and feel everything deeply. You may have a lot to express but have the good sense to process it all first. Uranus is bubbling inside your family sector and you may find a solution to a problem come up from nowhere. Your ego and emotions are in sync.

NOVEMBER

....

Monday 1st

You achieve more balance and look to outside activities to keep you afloat. Stretching your wings is natural for an air sign but grounding yourself is a problem. Educational studies can do this for you right now. Look for a new avenue to explore. This could become part of your current transformation.

Tuesday 2nd

Today you struggle as you fail to see that allowing yourself some down time is the best thing for you at the moment. Saturn supports you and asks you to see that your personal boundaries need strengthening. You don't have to be everything for everybody.

Wednesday 3rd

The Moon meets Mercury and you may find that you're going over and over certain thoughts and getting nowhere. Discuss this with someone you trust. You may experience some confusion as your road ahead looks very different from how you first imagined it. Trust that you will always be guided towards your best self.

Thursday 4th

The Moon meets Mars before becoming New in your career sector. This is time to review your social status and ask yourself if it's working for you. Transform or discard things that are weighing you down. You may find that you do this impulsively or very suddenly today.

Friday 5th

Venus has entered your hidden sector and will help you to love alone time more. Any inner work done while she's here will be tempered with compassion for yourself. Mercury moves into your high-flying career sector and will up the ante in your communication skills in the workplace.

Saturday 6th

The Moon shifts just in time for the weekend. A social event with your wider groups may be the perfect excuse to let off steam and party the night away. This may possibly be with work colleagues. Mercury talks to Venus about making subtle shifts at work. This might help alleviate some stress.

Sunday 7th

You have no time for dreaming today unless it's with friends who share your vision. You may be more inclined towards those who are outgoing and driven than those who are spiritual and ethereal. Plans for the upcoming festivities can excite you. You may have a leading role to play here.

Monday 8th

Today can have a seductive quality that you lap up and enjoy. The Moon meets Venus in your hidden sector and connects to Mars and the Sun. Passion and romance are favoured and there may be a secret rendezvous on the agenda. Something new gives you goosebumps.

Tuesday 9th

Pluto hosts the Moon for her monthly visit. You may find that you're emotionally attached to re-inventing yourself again. Now that you've come to terms with it, it sounds like the best thing you can do. Be patient as this may take some time.

Wednesday 10th

Heavy energy may drain you today. Although the Moon is in your sign, it connects poorly to other planets and you may feel restricted, fatigued and exposed. Mercury and Mars in your career sector may be responsible for high activity and a list of deadlines you need to meet before the week is out.

Thursday 11th

Your nerves may be frazzled and there's a possibility that you take it out on your nearest and dearest. Jupiter makes things larger and you may find that squabbles get out of control very quickly. Rein them in by being fluid and adaptable to any change that comes.

Friday 12th

A little help from Venus goes a long way today. You're mindful of the need to withdraw into yourself if things get too much. This would be a good time to pause and reflect on the year gone by. You may rediscover skills and talents that you can use again.

Saturday 13th

Be very careful what you say, you may inadvertently slip up and betray a confidence. Your mind is not on your job and you're at risk of drifting off. Your true north has gripped you and won't let go. Hang in there and enjoy the moment.

Sunday 14th

Water energy makes you more sensitive to other's needs. A new romance may be blossoming or is hidden behind a veil from the outside world. Is this a secret or are you being protective? How does this fit in with the new you? Is it part of your progress?

Monday 15th

You may be fired up with a list of chores to do. This might have an impact on your inner strength, and you may feel resentful that you have no time for yourself. Do your duty but no more, you'll have to be strong and say no.

Tuesday 16th

Today may be very busy as your communications sector is highlighted. There may be many messages to make or plans to negotiate. If you're doing something for a wider group, ensure that all the work doesn't fall on your shoulders. Share the love and share the workload.

Wednesday 17th

Volatile energy makes today very tricky for you. You may be caught in the crossfire of work and home problems. Nothing seems very easy at the moment and you are not enjoying home life as you should. You just want to get away from it all somehow.

Thursday 18th

The rollercoaster of managing work and home duties may come to a head today. Someone, maybe you, will have a tantrum and the tension will be broken. Know that this opens up lines of communication to resolve this problem. Mercury may win you round with promising words and dreams.

Friday 19th

There's a Full Moon in your family sector which will throw a spotlight on the recent tension and you may see that this has been coming for a long time. Venus talks nicely to Uranus and people may begin to see how negatively you've been affected by taking on all the work.

Saturday 20th

Take a day and use your creative talents to describe your emotions. You may not be able to get a grip on them any other way. Listening to music will be a great therapeutic exercise. Someone may try to bully you today, but they won't get far.

Sunday 21st

Artistic endeavours may feel blocked as the Moon squares off with dreamy Neptune. You have an urge to switch off from outside life and do your own thing. Pay a visit to someone you trust and have a heart to heart. This may be good for your self-esteem.

Monday 22nd

Today is far more nurturing. You recognise the need to do your everyday duties and leave time for yourself. A secret meeting or time spent with maternal figures will nourish your senses and make you feel good. Happiness is not hard to find now so grab it with both hands.

Tuesday 23rd

You may be enjoying time with a person who cares for you so much that you seem to forget how to care for yourself. Venus gives you a nudge and asks you to be on your guard. You may be excitable, unpredictable and too dreamy for your own good today.

Wednesday 24th

A sudden urge to break free tells you that you've had enough of being smothered with love for now. It may even feel controlling and this makes you revolt. You desire partner time where you feel you can show off and parade with someone who has more confidence than you.

Thursday 25th

Mars and Venus are making a helpful connection for would-be lovers. Perhaps this is done behind closed doors. Be careful as there may be some passive-aggressive behaviour going on and this coupling may, in fact, be rather toxic for you. Stand up and be seen. Be loud and proud.

Friday 26th

A fiery Moon in your relationship sector opposes Jupiter. What has the lucky planet seen and not agreed with? You may find that you've come to a sticking point, even if just momentarily. Do your partner's needs and visions meet your own? Review this question now.

Saturday 27th

Your heart and head are not in sync. There's no point trying to reconcile them as they won't agree. You may think that you're being flexible, but you're actually being non-committal. Give up trying for today and come back to it when the Moon shifts.

Sunday 28th

Today, you need answers. You've been through your inner filing cabinet and found gaps. You may be prepared to go the extra mile for a person you care about, but they're not being totally honest with you. Root out the cause of this and discuss things openly.

Monday 29th

Mercury is in the heart of the Sun and saying nothing. Your social sector may seem busy and superficial. It's your job to listen for subtle messages and look out for signposts. These may tell you something about how your wider groups are operating. Why have you missed this until now?

Tuesday 30th

The energy today suggests that you compare your agenda to those of people around you. They may seem to match but do they really? How might you ensure that personal boundaries aren't breached, and that each person has total respect from others? Make agreements or contracts within your groups.

DECEMBER

· · · · · · · · · · · · · · · · · ·

Wednesday 1st

The big news is that Neptune has turned direct. You may now get more in line with your inner compass. Remember that he resides in your money sector and you will need to hold on to your cash and not let it slip away. You can determine fantasies from real dreams now.

Thursday 2nd

The Moon opposes Uranus and you may see the familiar conflicts between your home and work lives. Responsibilities regarding both may be difficult to manage under this influence. You're more inclined to see to yourself first and others second. Be sure not to let people down today.

Friday 3rd

The Moon meets fiery Mars in your career sector. You may be rushing or extra motivated to finish up jobs and meet deadlines. This may put extra pressure on your duties to yourself and wider groups but will need to be done. Stay strong as this won't last long.

Saturday 4th

A New Moon in your social sector is a great chance to make plans that are big, bold and adventurous. Speak to your interest groups and get advice or ideas to stretch yourself in the next six months. Maybe a visit to a long-distance friend will suffice. Keep it real and do-able.

Sunday 5th

Make the most of Jupiter's energy in your sign before he leaves. Broaden your outlook and think about how different cultures and overseas trips might advance your knowledge and understanding of yourself. Take some time this evening to process your thoughts and make a game plan for the coming year.

Monday 6th

Today has great energy for you to access and use in all walks of life. You may be quietly planning surprises for the family whilst idly dreaming about your bigger vision. Mars and Pluto talk and help you to take action where appropriate and make changes that will be worthwhile.

Tuesday 7th

The Moon meets Pluto in your hidden sector. You may feel more positive this month and no longer feel that you're being threatened with too much change and adjustment. This afternoon the Moon drops into your sign and you can put your best foot forward and show up to life.

Wednesday 8th

You may need to pull back a little today and remember where your duties are. It's possible that you're trying to run before you can walk. Agitations from your home will likely be the reason for this. You desire to get going but there's a red light stopping you.

Thursday 9th

The Moon and Jupiter meet in your sign. You may find
that any tension will feel bigger than it needs to be. Stop,
pause and breathe before you do anything. Take in the wider
picture before acting. Find that altruistic side of you and
put others first.

Friday 10th

You may well be spending too much money today, but it will
be well spent. The Moon is in your money sector connecting
to Uranus in your home sector. This could be your festive
shopping day. Uranus likes surprises and so do you. You
especially like giving them to others.

Saturday 11th

Venus meets Pluto today in your hidden sector. This is
important as she will retrograde soon. Love, harmony and
beauty must be combined with change and transformation.
Perhaps you've had a change of heart about someone who you
believe has wronged you. Perhaps you're considering a whole
new you.

Sunday 12th

Today will be filled with communication of all sorts. There
may be many plans to be made for the festive season so get out
your planner and make sure you enter everything. You're very
happy when filling up your time. Check your bank balance
allows for this much activity.

Monday 13th

Mercury enters your hidden sector while Mars marches into your social sector. This heralds a time of hedonistic fun with friends and then reprimanding yourself when alone. You could overdo the good things in life now and fret about it later. Exercise some self-discipline.

Tuesday 14th

You may have trouble pleasing yourself as others demand too much of your attention. There's a possibility that you exhaust yourself for the sake of the family. Self-talk can be positive if you run your thoughts through the good reasons you have for doing this but remember to take care of your own needs too.

Wednesday 15th

The tension that comes with this season catches up with you. There may be conflict in the family. You can be stubborn and unmoving or quite the opposite and go too far with someone. Expect a blow-out of some sort as tempers may be frayed.

Thursday 16th

Today there's better energy which can help to soothe family squabbles. Your innermost thoughts are already transforming themselves to help you deal with the delicate balance of yours and others' needs. You may feel like hosting an early party tonight. Once again, you will need to curb your spending.

Friday 17th

The Moon sits opposite Mars and this energy can make you drained. Your emotional needs are to create, make love or music but your wider groups are calling for your presence. In this case, the groups will win as it's easier for you to let off steam with them.

Saturday 18th

You still have the creative buzz running within you and you may have time to do something about it today. A vision board for next year containing all the new plans and dreams you have will be a good exercise. You're adaptable and moody so use those feelings to create.

Sunday 19th

Venus turns retrograde. Over the next forty days, you may see an old lover return or your current one disappear. In your hidden sector, you may also see profound change from deep inside you. A Full Moon lights up your creative sector and puts your talents in the spotlight.

Monday 20th

This may be a lucky day with surprises coming your way. You may have the need to be nurtured and looked after but also a conflicting need to break free from confines. Feminine wisdom will come to you today and you need to listen. Something will trigger an old wound.

Tuesday 21st

The Winter Solstice takes place as the Sun enters your hidden sector. You may find this month uncomfortable as your innermost thoughts and processes may be revealed. Take this time to pause and reflect on the year gone by. Reward yourself for the hard work you have done.

Wednesday 22nd

Partner time may help you to come out of a quiet zone and give you freedom of speech. Choose someone you trust and relate to well. You may need to get things off your chest in a safe place. Be bold and brave as your relationship sector is highlighted.

Thursday 23rd

Today is another chance to pause. The Moon is safely in your relationship sector and you may enjoy time with a lover which is uninterrupted by outside influences. Jupiter is about to leave your sign; how can you thank the lucky planet for his stay? Can you do something brave?

Friday 24th

You may feel over-emotional and pull back from relating to others. You might feel the need to have a clear out or isolate yourself. Tension could arise in your family and social sectors. There are too many people demanding your attention and you desire to run and hide.

Saturday 25th

Try to stay grounded and as be as practical as possible today. The planetary energy supports this as the best way to get through the day. Issues surrounding self-care or ex-lovers may surface as Venus has retrograded back to meet Pluto. You may experience some subtle manipulation today.

· · · · · · · · · · · · · · · · · ·

Sunday 26th

The Moon connects to Venus and Pluto making you emotionally invested in whatever Venus retrograde has brought up for you. You deal with it responsibly and can decide to put it to one side for now. Your thought processes surrounding this are logical and you may begin to see another point of view.

Monday 27th

Today you can achieve more balance, but you may use distractions such as your friendship groups. Are you avoiding dealing with a nasty situation? Putting up a personal boundary and sticking to it may be a better way of handling this. Use your Mars energy to defend you.

Tuesday 28th

You may be feeling burnt out by recent activity and the best thing you can do is hide away with a good book. Your thoughts are doing overtime, your self-care is poor, and you feel victimised or manipulated. Say goodbye to Jupiter as he leaves your sign.

Wednesday 29th

Jupiter now enters your money and value house. This is a lucky sign if you're wishing to increase your financial situation. It's also beneficial as you'll start to see your own self-worth in a different way. You may be too hard on yourself today and this will need to change.

Thursday 30th

As the year draws to a close you may find that your thoughts are filled with your dreams for the future and your inner transformation. Mercury meets Pluto and they discuss your progress so far. The next stage of your development is about to begin.

Friday 31st

The Moon meets up with Mars in your social sector which is just the energy you need for a great festive celebration with friends. You may look back on the year gone by and vow to honour the heavy demands of your ruler Saturn as he strives to make you a better person.

Aquarius

. . . .

PEOPLE WHO SHARE
YOUR SIGN

PEOPLE WHO
SHARE YOUR SIGN

· · · · · · · · · · · · · · · · ·

Born to be different and shake things up, Aquarians are the liberating Air sign that are prepared to ruffle some feathers if needed. From the speeches of Abraham Lincoln to the words of Virginia Woolf, the unique insight and intellect that so many Aquarians have make them a sign to be listened to and take notice of. Discover which of these individualist Aquarians share your exact birthday with and see if you can spot the similarities.

21st January

BooBoo Stewart (1994), Jerry Trainor (1977), Emma Bunton (1976), Geena Davis (1956), Paul Allen (1953), Billy Ocean (1950), Plácido Domingo (1941), Benny Hill (1924), Christian Dior (1905), Grigori Rasputin (1869)

22nd January

Silentó (1998), Logic (1990), Hidetoshi Nakata (1977), Gabriel Macht (1972), Guy Fieri (1968), Diane Lane (1965), Linda Blair (1959), Steve Perry (1949), John Hurt (1940)

23rd January

Doutzen Kroes (1985), Draya Michele (1985), Arjen Robben (1984), Tito Ortiz (1975), Tiffani Thiessen (1974), Mariska Hargitay (1964), Princess Caroline of Hanover (1957), Richard Dean Anderson (1950), Édouard Manet (1832)

24th January

Luis Suárez (1987), Mischa Barton (1986), Justin Baldoni (1984), Frankie Grande (1983), Tatyana Ali (1979), Kristen Schaal (1978), Ed Helms (1974), Kenya Moore (1971), Sharon Tate (1943)

25th January

Calum Hood (1996), Robinho (1984), Alicia Keys (1981), Xavi (1980), Princess Charlene of Monaco (1978), Virginia Woolf (1882)

26th January

Colin O'Donoghue (1981), Brendan Rodgers (1973), José Mourinho (1963), Wayne Gretzky (1961), Ellen DeGeneres (1958), Eddie Van Halen (1955), Angela Davis (1944), Paul Newman (1925), Louis Zamperini (1917), Maria von Trapp (1905)

27th January

Rosamund Pike (1979), Patton Oswalt (1969), Alan Cumming (1965), Bridget Fonda (1964), Narciso Rodriguez (1961), Mimi Rogers (1956), Mikhail Baryshnikov (1948), Beatrice Tinsley (1941), Lewis Carroll (1832)

28th January

Ariel Winter (1998), Will Poulter (1993), J. Cole (1985), Elijah Wood (1981), Nick Carter (1980), Gianluigi Buffon (1978), Rick Ross (1976), Carlos Slim (1940), Alan Alda (1936)

29th January

Adam Lambert (1982), Sara Gilbert (1975), Heather Graham (1970), Oprah Winfrey (1954), Tom Selleck (1945), Katharine Ross (1940), Anton Chekhov (1860)

30th January

Eiza González (1990), Arda Turan (1987), Wilmer Valderrama (1980), Christian Bale (1974), Phil Collins (1951), Dick Cheney, U.S. Vice President (1941), Franklin D. Roosevelt, U.S. President (1882)

31st January

Amy Jackson (1992), Marcus Mumford (1987), Justin Timberlake (1981), Kerry Washington (1977), Portia de Rossi (1973), Minnie Driver (1970), Daniel Moder (1969), John Lydon (1956), Jonathan Banks (1947), Carol Channing (1921), Jackie Robinson (1919), Baba Vanga (1911)

1st February

Harry Styles (1994), Heather Morris (1987), Ronda Rousey (1987), Lauren Conrad (1986), Abbi Jacobson (1984), Michael C. Hall (1971), Lisa Marie Presley (1968), Princess Stéphanie of Monaco (1965), Langston Hughes (1902), Clark Gable (1901)

2nd February

Gerard Piqué (1987), Gemma Arterton (1986), Gemma Collins (1981), Christine Bleakley (1979), Shakira (1977), Christie Brinkley (1954), Duncan Bannatyne (1949), Farrah Fawcett (1947), David Jason (1940), Ayn Rand (1905), James Joyce (1882)

3rd February

Sean Kingston (1990), Elizabeth Holmes (1984), Amal Clooney (1978), Isla Fisher (1976), Warwick Davis (1970), Maura Tierney (1965), Joachim Löw (1960), Nathan Lane (1956), Blythe Danner (1943), Norman Rockwell (1894)

4th February

Hannibal Buress (1983), Gavin DeGraw (1977), Cam'ron (1976), Natalie Imbruglia (1975), Oscar De La Hoya (1973), Alice Cooper (1948), Rosa Parks (1913), Charles Lindbergh (1902)

5th February

Neymar (1992), Darren Criss (1987), Kevin Gates (1986), Cristiano Ronaldo (1985), Carlos Tevez (1984), Tiwa Savage (1980), Bobby Brown (1969), Michael Sheen (1969), Laura Linney (1964), Duff McKagan (1964), Jennifer Jason Leigh (1962)

6th February

Tinashe (1993), Dane DeHaan (1986), Alice Eve (1982), Rick Astley (1966), Axl Rose (1962), Kathy Najimy (1957), Bob Marley (1945), Ronald Reagan, U.S. President (1911), Babe Ruth (1895)

7th February

Bea Miller (1999), Jacksepticeye (1990), Deborah Ann Woll (1985), Ashton Kutcher (1978), Chris Rock (1965), Garth Brooks (1962), Eddie Izzard (1962), James Spader (1960), Laura Ingalls Wilder (1876), Charles Dickens (1812)

8th February

Klay Thompson (1990), Seth Green (1974), Mauricio Macri, Argentinian President (1959), Mary Steenburgen (1953), John Williams (1932), James Dean (1931), Dmitri Mendeleev (1834), Jules Verne (1828)

9th February

Michael B. Jordan (1987), Rose Leslie (1987), Tom Hiddleston (1981), Zhang Ziyi (1979), Charlie Day (1976), Amber Valletta (1974), Chris Gardner (1954), Mia Farrow (1945), Alice Walker (1944), Joe Pesci (1943), Carole King (1942)

10th February

Chloë Grace Moretz (1997), Emma Roberts (1991), Radamel Falcao (1986), Uzo Aduba (1981), Stephanie Beatriz (1981), Holly Willoughby (1981), Don Omar (1978), Elizabeth Banks (1974), Laura Dern (1967), Bertolt Brecht (1898)

11th February

Taylor Lautner (1992), Natalie Dormer (1982), Kelly Rowland (1981), Damian Lewis (1971), Jennifer Aniston (1969), Sarah Palin (1964), Sheryl Crow (1962), Burt Reynolds (1936), Leslie Nielsen (1926), Thomas Edison (1847)

12th February

Mike Posner (1988), Iko Uwais (1983), Gucci Mane (1980), Christina Ricci (1980), Naseem Hamed (1974), Josh Brolin (1968), Chris McCandless (1968), Charles Darwin (1809), Abraham Lincoln, U.S. President (1809)